Epworth Commen

General Editor
Ivor H. Jones

The Epistle of James

Epworth Commentaries

Already published

The Book of Job
C. S. Rodd

Isaiah 1–39
David Stacey

The Books of Amos and Hosea
Harry Mowvley

The Gospel of John
Kenneth Grayston

The First Epistle to the Corinthians
Nigel Watson

The Second Epistle to the Corinthians
Nigel Watson

The Epistle to the Galatians
John Ziesler

The Epistle to the Philippians
Howard Marshall

The Epistle to the Colossians
Roy Yates

The Epistle to the Hebrews
Paul Ellingworth

The Johannine Epistles
William Loader

Revelation
Christopher Rowland

In preparation

I and II Thessalonians
Neil Richardson

The Epistle of
JAMES

Michael J. Townsend

EPWORTH PRESS

Extracts from the Revised English Bible are © 1989
by the Delegates of the Oxford University Press and the
Syndics of the Cambridge University Press and are used
by permission

ISBN 0 7162 0500 9

First Published 1994
by Epworth Press
1 Central Buildings Westminster
London SW1H 9NR

Typeset by Regent Typesetting, London
Printed and bound in Finland by
Werner Söderström Oy

CONTENTS

GENERAL INTRODUCTION

The *Epworth Preacher's Commentaries* that Greville P. Lewis edited so successfully in the 1950s and 1960s having now served their turn, the Epworth Press has commissioned a team of distinguished academics who are also preachers and teachers to create a new series of commentaries that will serve the 1990s and beyond. We have seized the opportunity offered by the publication in 1989 of the Revised English Bible to use this very readable and scholarly version as the basis of our commentaries, and we are grateful to the Oxford and Cambridge University Presses for the requisite licence and for granting our authors pre-publication access. They will nevertheless be free to cite and discuss other translations wherever they think that these will illuminate the original text.

Just as the books that make up the Bible differ in their provenance and purpose, so our authors will necessarily differ in the structure and bearing of their commentaries. But they will all strive to get as close as possible to the intention of the original writers, expounding their texts in the light of the place, time, circumstances, and culture that gave them birth, and showing why each work was received by Jews and Christians into their respective Canons of Holy Scripture. They will seek to make full use of the dramatic advance in biblical scholarship world-wide but at the same time to explain technical terms in the language of the common reader, and to suggest ways in which Scripture can help towards the living of a Christian life today. They will endeavour to produce commentaries that can be used with confidence in ecumenical, multiracial, and multifaith situations, and not by scholars only but by preachers, teachers, students, church members, and anyone who wants to improve his or her understanding of the Bible.

Ivor H. Jones

PREFACE

The appearance of this commentary from the pen of one who does not claim to be an NT specialist, might seem to call for some explanation. I can only plead that I have had a considerable interest in the Epistle of James for a good many years, to the extent of drafting a commentary on it during some spare time on a five-month course in Switzerland in 1972–3. The script of that was mercifully lost a long time ago, but over the years since I have tried to keep up with the most important publications concerning James. I am therefore extremely grateful to the Editorial Committee of the Epworth Press for being willing to entrust me with the present work. I write as one who works as a pastor, preacher and teacher in the life of the church, which may be thought not entirely inappropriate for a commentator on this particular book (James 3.1). My considerable dependence on the work of real scholars will be everywhere apparent, but I hope that what I have written will be useful for those for whom the Epworth Commentaries are particularly designed.

In a commentary of this length it is not possible to interact with all the scholarly literature on the subject, nor to review every interpretation of the text which has ever been offered. In those passages where several plausible views exist concerning the meaning of the text I have tried to indicate what these are, so that the reader can make up his or her own mind on the basis of the evidence. At the same time, I have not hesitated to indicate where my own preferences lie. The Notes at the end of the Commentary are intended to have two purposes: (i) to indicate my own specific indebtedness to the work of others and, occasionally, my disagreement and (ii) to suggest where fuller treatments of important points may be found.

The completion of this Commentary has been undertaken during a sabbatical, October–December 1993. I feel extremely privileged to serve a church which allows its ministers such an opportunity every seven years, and doubt that the project would otherwise have been completed. I am grateful to the staff of the John Rylands Library at the University of Manchester and the Brotherton and Holden

Libraries at the University of Leeds for their unfailing courtesy and helpfulness. Much is also owed to the editor of the Epworth Commentaries, Dr Ivor H. Jones, for his patient and thorough help and advice, though he bears no responsibility for any of my conclusions. I owe a particular debt of gratitude to the members of my Sabbatical Support Group: Revd Eileen Appleyard, Mr John Garner, Mr Allen Illingworth, Dr Jean Lightbody, Mrs Pat Mudd and Mrs Barbara Swallow. Their careful planning ensured that I was able to enter on the sabbatical period free from anxiety about how my normal work would be handled in my absence. The knowledge that the day-to-day administration of the Huddersfield Mission was in the capable hands of our Secretary, Mrs Dorothy Normanton, helped to keep me free from such anxiety and able to concentrate on James! It is to them, and to the members of the Huddersfield Mission who, during five years of stimulating and rewarding ministry, have taught me something of what it means to be a church both of and for the poor, that this commentary is dedicated.

ABBREVIATIONS USED

(Other than for books of the Bible)

ATR	*Anglican Theological Review*
AV	Authorised Version (King James Bible)
BDB	F. Brown, S.R. Driver, C.A. Briggs, *A Hebrew and English Lexicon of the Old Testament*, Clarendon Press, Oxford 1907
Bib	*Biblica*
BJRL	*Bulletin of the John Rylands Library*
CBQ	*Catholic Biblical Quarterly*
Ecclus.	Ecclesiasticus
EQ	*Evangelical Quarterly*
ET	English Translation
ExT	*Expository Times*
GNB	Good News Bible
Gk	Greek
HTR	*Harvard Theological Review*
Ibid.	The work cited in the previous reference
INT	*Interpretation*
JB	Jerusalem Bible
JBL	*Journal of Biblical Literature*
JSNT	*Journal for the Study of the New Testament*
JSS	*Journal of Semitic Studies*
JTS	*Journal of Theological Studies*
ms(s)	manuscript(s)
NEB	New English Bible
Neot	*Neotestamentica*
NIV	New International Version
NJB	New Jerusalem Bible
NovT	*Novum Testamentum*
NRSV	New Revised Standard Version
NT	New Testament
NTS	*New Testament Studies*
op.cit.	The work by the same author cited in this section of the notes.

OT	Old Testament
REB	Revised English Bible
RSV	Revised Standard Version
RV	Revised Version
SE	*Studia Evangelica*
SJT	*Scottish Journal of Theology*
ST	*Studia theologica*
VE	*Vox Evangelica*
Wisd.	The Wisdom of Solomon
ZNW	*Zeitschrift für die neutestamentliche Wissenschaft*

A SELECT LIST OF COMMENTARIES ON JAMES

Only works in English are included in the following list, or referred to in the text of the Commentary, although others have been consulted during its preparation. Even at this date we could do with a translation of F. Mussner's excellent 1964 commentary which remains in German, though many of its most useful points have been culled by later writers in English. Where works are co-published in more than one country the British edition is listed.

Commentaries on the Greek text

P. H. Davids, *The Epistle of James*, New International Greek Testament Commentaries, Paternoster Press, Exeter 1982.

F. J. A. Hort, *The Epistle of St. James*, Macmillan, London 1909 (only as far as 4.7).

R. P. Martin, *James*, Word Bible Commentary 48, Word Books, Waco, Texas 1988.

J. B. Mayor, *The Epistle of St. James*, 3rd edn. rev., Macmillan, London 1913.

J. H. Ropes, *The Epistle of St. James*, International Critical Commentary, T. &T. Clark, Edinburgh 1916.

Commentaries on the English text

J. B. Adamson, *The Epistle of James*, New International Commentary on the New Testament, Eerdmans, Grand Rapids, Michigan 1976.

E. C. Blackman, *The Epistle of James*, Torch Bible Commentaries, SCM Press, London 1957.

P. H. Davids, *James*, New International Bible Commentaries, Hendrickson, Peabody, Mass. 1989.

M. Dibelius, *James: A Commentary on the Epistle of James*, 11th edn., revised H. Greeven, ET, Hermeneia, Fortress Press, Philadelphia 1976 (original commentary 1920).

R. Kugelman, *James and Jude*, Veritas, Dublin 1980.

S. Laws, *The Epistle of James*, Black's New Testament Commentaries, A. & C. Black, London 1980.

C. L. Mitton, *The Epistle of James*, Marshall Morgan and Scott, London 1966.

J. Moffatt, *The General Epistles of James, Peter and Jude*, Moffat New Testament Commentaries, Hodder and Stoughton, London 1928.

D. J. Moo, *The Letter of James*, Tyndale New Testament Commentaries, IVP, Leicester 1985.

B. Reicke, *The Epistles of James, Peter and Jude*, Anchor Bible, Doubleday and Co., New York 1964.

E. M. Sidebottom, *James, Jude and II Peter*, New Century Bible, Nelson, London 1967.

G. Stulac, *James*, IVP New Testament Commentaries, Leicester 1993.

R. V. G. Tasker, *The General Epistle of James*, Tyndale New Testament Commentaries, Tyndale Press, London 1957.

R. R. Williams, *The Letters of John and James*, Cambridge Bible Commentaries, CUP, Cambridge 1965.

INTRODUCTION

General

Many years ago, the BBC Third Programme (as Radio 3 was then called) offered a programme entitled 'The Innocent Ear'. Pieces of music were played, but listeners were told neither the title nor the composer until after they had been heard. In this way it was hoped to overcome some of the prejudices and expectations many of us bring with us when we listen to music, and also perhaps to surprise listeners by playing a composition they enjoyed by a composer whose music they had previously thought they disliked. However, despite the good intentions, an 'innocent ear' proved an impossibility. Although the listener might not previously have heard the piece in question, he or she had heard *other* pieces of music. It became difficult not to turn the programme into a guessing game, trying to work out what was being played by attending to such matters as harmony and instrumentation. Even so, there was value in the exercise; at the very least it developed the listener's capacity to discern musical styles and to listen carefully both for influences and for those more personal stylistic traits developed by particular composers. When we begin to study an NT document we are engaged in a similar process. It is almost impossible to approach it with an innocent ear. If we have not read it for a long time, or even if we have never read it before, we come to it with some idea that we know what it is about. In the course of our study we make comparisons with other writings that we do know. As a result of so doing, we also begin to recognize the characteristics which belong uniquely to the document we are studying. What then, might a relatively innocent reader make of James on a first encounter?

Imagine someone undertaking a serious reading of the Bible for the first time beginning with Genesis, someone who was also blessed with an exceptionally retentive memory. What might such a person say on first reading the Epistle of James? Perhaps something like this: 'In some ways it is quite unlike anything else I have read, in other respects it reminds me of several things. In places it recalls those parts of the Old Testament which stress the importance of keeping God's laws – such as Leviticus. In other places it is reminiscent of the way in which some of the prophets denounce injustice. At times it reminds me of those books in the Old Testament which contain the sayings of wise people, such as Proverbs. Yet it obviously belongs in the New Testament rather than the Old, not only because it mentions Jesus a couple of times, but because it seems to echo some of the sayings of Jesus I read in the gospels, particularly in Matthew. It is called an 'epistle', but it isn't quite like most of the other epistles I have read, especially those by Paul. I am not quite sure what to make of it, but it is certainly different!' If our imaginary 'innocent reader' had also previously read some of what is called the 'wisdom literature' of later Judaism, he or she would also notice many echoes of that in James. These are indeed the 'puzzles' which confront us in this epistle. It is a writing springing from the rich soil of first-century AD Judaism. To what extent is it nourished by Christian theology and, if it is, why is this not more explicitly stated? It clearly has some relationship with the teaching of Jesus as it is now recorded in the first three gospels, but what kind of relationship is this? Did the writer (whoever he may have been) know anything of the theology of Paul? Was it perhaps the other way round, or did they write quite independently? Against what kind of background was James written, for whom, and when? Is it an epistle and, if not, what kind of writing is it? Many of these questions apply to other NT documents, but in the case of the Epistle of James the range of possible answers which have been offered is wider than for almost any other NT writing.

If James resists easy classification, its presence in the biblical canon ought to serve as a constant reminder that the NT writings cannot be homogenized into a bland product called 'New Testament theology'. It ought also to act as a check on any ready resort to the phrase, 'the Bible says', and it reminds us that the theologies of Paul, and of the Johannine community from which the Fourth Gospel emerged, even though these dominate the New Testament, were not the only responses to the life, death and resurrection of Jesus. Other groups of Christians also made their response and re-evaluated their religious traditions and beliefs in the light of what they believed God had done in Christ. We may see James as the witness to one such response, and should cherish it for its individuality.

Unfortunately, Christians have not always cherished the Epistle of James. In relatively modern times its reputation has suffered from the views of the great German Reformer, Martin Luther (1483–1546). Luther is often quoted as calling James an 'epistle of straw', but the fuller context of that remark is worth exploring. In the Preface to his translation of the Bible into German, Luther lists what he describes as the 'truest and noblest books of the New Testament' (in his opinion, John, Romans and I Peter), records all the books that 'show you Christ and teach you all that is necessary and salvatory for you to know, even if you were never to see or hear any other book or doctrine' and adds: 'Therefore St James' epistle is really an epistle of straw, compared to these others, for it has nothing of the nature of the gospel about it.'[1] However, in his 'Preface to James and Jude' we appear to find a more favourable judgement: 'Though this epistle of St James was rejected by the ancients, I praise it and consider it a good book, because it sets up no doctrine of men but vigorously promulgates the law of God.'[2] Luther is here being either inconsistent or ironic, because he continues with an assessment which hardly constitutes 'praise'. He writes: 'it is flatly against St Paul', and complains that it does not mention the passion or resurrection of Christ, nor the Spirit. In short, it does not inculcate Christ and, 'whatever does not teach Christ is not yet apostolic, even though St Peter or St Paul do the teaching.' And so, 'this James does nothing more than drive to the law and to its works.' In a further scathing attack he appears to anticipate some twentieth-century critical judgements about the date and form of James: 'Besides, he throws some things together so chaotically that it seems to me he must have been some good, pious man, who took a few sayings from the disciples of the apostles and thus tossed them off on paper. Or it may perhaps have been written by someone on the basis of his preaching.'[3] Other Reformers, it is true, did not share Luther's judgement. John (or Jean) Calvin (1509–1564) had a much more balanced assessment to offer. Far from sharing Luther's view that James is 'flatly against St Paul', he wrote that 'it is surely not required of all to handle the same arguments . . . but this diversity should not make us to approve of one, and to condemn the other.'[4] On the whole it is Luther's view which has prevailed in Western Protestantism, at least until recent times. This has, perhaps, been reflected in the level of interest in this document amongst NT scholars. During a period of twenty-five years or so at the end of the nineteenth and beginning of the twentieth centuries, several commentaries were written on James which are indispensable even today, but that was followed by a lengthy period of neglect. In recent years, as we have come to appreciate more and more of the unity and diversity of the NT, interest in James has revived and today there is a healthy flow of new works, both articles and commentaries, to help us understand this fascinating, if sometimes baffling epistle. Of course, the contemporary Christian will hardly turn to James for a fully balanced diet of theology. But there is more theology in this writing than it has sometimes been given credit for, and in addition to its major emphasis on practical action, the Epistle of James makes its own distinctive contribution to the faith of Jesus, the Lord and the Glory, whose brothers and sisters we are through the gospel.[5]

The nature of the document

When is an epistle not an epistle? Many writers have given as the answer to that question: when it is the Epistle of James! True, the document appears to open as we expect a Greek letter to do, with a conventional statement about who is sending it and who are the recipients, but there it seems, the resemblance ends. Like I John, but unlike other NT letters, it carries no blessing or salutation at the close, and the end comes somewhat abruptly. The addressees are not a specific church or group of churches, nor an individual but 'the twelve tribes dispersed throughout the world' (1.1). This sounds both general and relatively impersonal, so even the opening, conventional though it appears to be, raises some doubts about whether a real letter is going to follow. But if James is not a letter, what are the alternatives?

The distinguished commentator J. H. Ropes argued that the document is cast in the form of a Greek diatribe.[6] In modern English we use the word diatribe to describe a sustained attack, often with implications of abuse ('she launched into a diatribe against her political enemies'), but that is not what the word meant in the world of Greek culture. Diatribes were addresses or lectures of an ethical or philosophical kind. They were known in the time of Socrates (469–399 BC) and developed by Diogenes (400–325 BC) and his followers, reaching a state of high art with Bion the Borysthenite (*c*.325 – *c*.255 BC). By the beginning of the Christian era the form was in common use by the Stoic philosophers, most notably Seneca (*c*.4 BC – AD 65) and Epictetus (*c*.AD 55 – *c*.135). The diatribe form had a long and sophisticated history and we need not be surprised if the early Christians made use of it. Some of the most characteristic traits of diatribe were set out by Ropes, along with suggested parallels in

James. The most important are: (i) Dialogue with an imaginary questioner, coupled with a brief question and answer form (2.18f. and 5.13f.); (ii) the making of a transition from one topic to another by raising an objection (2.8), by a question (2.14; 4.1; 5.13) or with a Greek word which the REB translates as 'now' (4.13) and 'next' (5.1); (iii) rhetorical questions, to which no answers are expected because they have already been supplied (2.4; 2.5; 2.14–16; 3.11ff.; 4.4ff.); (iv) personifications (1.15; 2.13; 4.1; 5.3f.); (v) the use of historical examples (Abraham, Rahab, Job, Elijah) and (vi) a general awareness on the part of the writer that he is not so much stating new truths as reminding readers of what is already familiar to them. Ropes recognized that there are some differences too, most notably in the seriousness of manner and more restrained tone which James adopts, in contrast to some of the Greek diatribes which have come down to us, but overall he had no doubt that James is a diatribe, having 'only the form' of a letter. The comparisons remain illuminating, but he claimed too much. There is no objection in principle to suggesting that the diatribe form has influenced James, or indeed other NT writers. Elements of diatribe style have often been thought to be present in some of Paul's writings too (notably Rom. 3.1–20), but it is a rather different matter to claim that the whole document is written in the form of a diatribe. Some scholars have questioned whether the diatribe ever existed as a literary *genre*[7] but that may be going too far.

Nearly fifty years ago, Albert Wifstrand pointed out that the evidence for calling James a diatribe is shaky; indeed, he called it a 'grotesque overstatement' to do so.[8] Some of the stylistic resemblances prove little. Certainly there are rhetorical questions in James, but so there are in the Book of Job. Personifications and the use of historical examples are indeed often cited in diatribes and found in James, but they are also found in the literature of Judaism. The one alleged resemblance between the diatribe and James which has no direct parallel in Jewish literature is the occurrence of objections from an imaginary questioner, but even here we need to remember that such a literary device was not exclusive to the diatribe form. On the whole though, it does seem likely that 'the diatribe heard in the streets and the market-places directly or indirectly has supplied these features to the author of the Epistle'[9] or even that some characteristics of the diatribe form had penetrated into the general usage of the synagogue sermon.[10] That is a very long way from saying that James *is* a diatribe.

Another term which has been often applied to James is 'parenesis' (sometimes spelled 'paraenesis'). Martin Dibelius, a highly influential commentator on James, did much to popularize this idea. He defined parenesis as: 'a text which strings together admonitions of general ethical content'.[11] Again, we are familiar with this kind of writing from the letters of Paul, where an ethical or parenetic section sometimes follows earlier and more explicitly theological material. The Epistle to the Romans provides the outstanding example, where a largely ethical or parenetic section begins at 12.1, following the theological wrestlings of the first eleven chapters. The situation with James however, is somewhat different. Whatever traditional ethical teaching Paul's letters may sometimes incorporate, it is nearly always possible to trace the impress of his own considerable mind upon them, and to observe the way in which he has shaped such materials to reflect and respond to his theological themes. It is less immediately evident in James that there is a clear theological mind at work. Identifying the author's own concerns and theological outlook is no easy task. The document is not laid out in a clear pattern of theological reflection followed by ethical exhortation; the moral and ethical considerations appear throughout the writing and dominate its concerns. Given that many of the teachings in James have been paralleled both from the Jewish Wisdom tradition and from collections of ethical maxims and instructions current in the world of Hellenistic culture, the writer of James appears as a snapper-up of unconsidered trifles, certainly more a compiler than an author. This was Dibelius' view, as it was that of Luther before him.

What are the characteristic features of parenesis which might lead to such a conclusion? One writer identifies five such features, and links them with James as follows: (i) the material is traditional and unoriginal, which fits James' use of the words of Jesus, the OT writings and Hellenistic Jewish literature; (ii) the material is generally applicable rather than written for a specific situation, which appears to be true of James; (iii) the material contains admonitions often addressed to one who knows them and has heard them before, which might be the case in James (1.19–27; 4.13–17); (iv) the material offers examples to be emulated, as James does with Abraham, Rahab, Job and Elijah; (v) the material displays a close relationship between the writer who is offering the teaching and those who are receiving it, and such a relationship surfaces a number of times in James (1.2; 2.1; 2.14; 3.1; 3.12; 5.7; 5.9; 5.12). All this leads to the conclusion that in James we have instruction given by a teacher at a time when he is either separated from his audience, or is about to leave them because of increasing age and approaching death.[12] Again, valuable though it is to look at James through this particular pair of interpretative spectacles, it must be said that as a *total* interpretation it also claims too much. Certainly James contains much parenetic material, but it is not as eclectic as it appears. Nor indeed is the material as free-floating and lacking in reference to a specific situation as has sometimes been assumed.[13] The epistle does indeed offer specific examples for the readers to emulate, but as we have already seen, so does the Jewish tradition. It is true that a number of the expressions in James suggest a close relationship with the readers, but this could also be claimed for the tone of those of Paul's letters which he wrote to churches which he had founded or helped to found. When we add to this the fact that many scholars now believe Dibelius was mistaken in thinking that parenesis was in itself a literary *genre*, it seems better to see James as a work with strong ethical concerns, making use of parenetic materials, but not limited to them. If then James is neither a diatribe nor a typically eclectic Hellenistic parenetic writing, the question of what it is still remains. Leaving aside such curiosities of biblical exegesis as the ingenious, though misplaced, attempt to show that it is a midrashic[14] composition based on Ps.12 with both the biblical references and the midrashic techniques eliminated,[15] we are left with three serious possibilities: a sermon, a literary tract or a pastoral letter.

At least since Luther's time, the suggestion that James is 'sermonic' has cropped up regularly in discussion, though often in a tentative manner. One commentator recollects a visiting preacher in his school chapel who described James as 'a collection of sermon notes' – a description he found inadequate, but suggestive and containing more than a modicum of truth.[16] Another commentator (assuming the material went back to James of Jerusalem) offers the not unattractive conjecture that visitors to Jerusalem, preparing to return home, wishing to have some written record of the teaching they had heard from the Lord's brother, compiled a selection from his sermons, and this is the document we now have.[17] One distinguished NT scholar, trying to account for the fact that there is little theological teaching in the epistle, suggests that it is based on a sermon, adding, 'it is quite possible that, on some occasions, the preacher might assume the Gospel and concentrate on ethical teaching.'[18] More recently it has been argued that the background of James must be sought in the Jewish synagogue sermon, which 'it would be perfectly natural for James to have adopted' for use in the church.[19] This may be so, but we cannot be sure. Most of the available evidence concerning the nature of Jewish synagogue sermons comes from after the Fall of Jerusalem in AD 70, and we really do not know whether or not that cataclysmic event ushered in a new style of preaching. Neither is there a great deal of evidence for the nature of Christian preaching in the early decades of the church's life. There are not many sermons in the NT documents; even if those recorded in the Acts of the Apostles accurately reflect what was actually said (which would be by no means universally agreed), they are clearly too much in the nature of occasional pieces, tailored to their specific circumstances, to allow us to make wider deductions about the content and style of Christian preaching in general. Attractive though these suggestions are, it must be reluctantly admitted that they rest on somewhat slender evidence.

What of the notion that James is a literary epistle, a tract intended for general publication rather than a letter comparable with those Paul wrote to specific churches? The frequently repeated judgement that James cannot be *any* kind of an epistle does indeed need to be questioned. As we have already seen, James shares certain features with I John, and it precisely these two documents which have been given a detailed examination by F. O. Francis. He concludes that they both have carefully styled thematic statements at the beginning, a recognizable epistolary close (especially in terms of subject matter) and an overall coherence. He chooses to designate both documents 'secondary epistles'.[20] If James is a literary epistle that would certainly help to account for its lack of greetings and personal details. More importantly, it would mean that the *Sitz im Leben*[21] of the document would be the place where it was written and issued rather than the place or places where it was received and read.[22] This is an important point and merits a little expansion. Many of the NT epistles were occasioned, in whole or in part, by difficulties or problems in particular churches. When Paul writes to the Galatians, for example, he begins by issuing sharp rebukes to them for having listened to some people (whose identity we do not know for sure) who have persuaded them that their salvation is incomplete. It is only as the argument of Galatians unfolds that we begin to learn more precisely the nature of what Paul describes as a 'different gospel' (Gal.1.6) and which so alarms him. It is thus perfectly clear that if the Galatian Christians had never received a visit from other preachers, or if they had rejected the teaching they were offered and kept to the understanding of the Christian faith as Paul had originally taught it to them, we would never have had the Epistle to the Galatians as it now stands. In other words, it is the circumstances of the recipients which determines the nature of the writing. When we try to read James in this way, we run into difficulties. It is not easy to envisage circumstances, situations or problems in particular churches which could call forth the variety of issues covered by James. The document becomes much more understandable however, if we envisage the writer setting forth his understanding of how the Christian life is to be lived against the background of the situation he knows best: the social, economic and political circumstances in which his own home congregation has to exercise its discipleship. This is not, of course, the same as saying that his concerns are *limited* to those of his home church. The epistle is a general one, addressed to those of his fellow Jewish Christians who value his guidance and help in understanding what it means to live by the 'law that makes us free' (1.25) and James does not hesitate to use material and language which would have been familiar to his readers.

Some have wished to go further than this, contending that James is a 'quasi-prophetic letter of pastoral encouragement, and, no less, of pastoral rebuke',[23] even that in this respect it should be aligned with Galatians or, especially, I Corinthians.[24] Though such arguments gloss over too many difficulties to be convincing, they do have the merit of reminding us that James is no coldly dispassionate literary production. It is written with vigour and verve and the writer clearly *feels* very deeply about his topics. In the final reckoning it probably does not matter too much what terminology we use to describe the Epistle of James. There are indeed many points of similarity between it and all sorts of styles and *genres* of writing (which is why so many different descriptions of it have been possible), but in the end we have to take it as it is, difficult to classify or pin down, but indisputably alive and vibrant. Whatever description of the nature of the document we are inclined to adopt, we must not allow it to determine our exegesis. The important thing is to attend to the text and what it has to say. There are two important matters which any reading of James brings to our attention: the relationship between the teaching of James and the teaching of Paul, and the relationship between the teaching of James and the teaching of Jesus. As these require more extended treatment than would be possible in the commentary itself we now turn to them.

James and Paul

Martin Luther's description of James as being 'flatly against St Paul' has tended to set the agenda with which students of the NT approach the epistle. It is a slight exaggeration to say that James 'continues to be studied almost entirely in terms of its relationship with Paul',[25] although where this is so the distinctive contribution James has to make to our understanding of the Christian gospel is lost. Nevertheless, the problem is a real one which can be stated more simply than it can be solved. In his letter to the Romans Paul writes: 'For no human being can be justified in the sight of God by keeping the law: law brings only the consciousness of sin' (Rom.3.20) and: 'our argument is that people are justified by faith quite apart from any question of keeping the law' (Rom.3.28). James on the other hand writes: 'Do you have to be told, you fool, that faith divorced from action is futile?' (James.2.20) and: 'You see then that it is by action and not by faith alone that a man is justified' (James.2.24). On the face of it this certainly looks like flat contradiction! The problem is compounded by the fact that Paul and James both use the example of Abraham to illustrate their arguments. For James it appears that Abraham's offering of his son Isaac on the altar (Gen. 22.1–18) was the action which justified Abraham in God's sight (James.2.21–23). Paul, on the other hand, devotes the whole of Romans 4 to arguing that Abraham's faith was counted to him as righteousness quite apart from any actions he performed.

How, if at all, may this be resolved? There are, broadly speaking, four positions which have been adopted on this, not all of them necessarily mutually exclusive. 1. Paul deliberately opposes and corrects what James teaches. This is not a view which finds much scholarly support[26] and the obvious difficulty with it is that in 2.14–26 James does not appear to be writing theoretically. The tone of the writing strongly suggestions a response to a genuine problem which some argue could not have arisen apart from Paul's teaching, or at least from a major misunderstanding of it. 2. James deliberately opposes and corrects Paul. This is not in principle impossible, and the view that James' argument presupposes that of Paul is a strong one.[27] It is extremely doubtful however, that James knew and was responding to the Epistle to the Romans (AD 57). If he was, then he made a poor job of it. 3. James was reacting to misunderstandings of Paul's teaching current in some of the churches to which he was writing. One difficulty with this is that it appears to demand a fairly late date for the Epistle of James, in order to fit a situation where, presumably several years after Paul's death, his teaching had become misunderstood. If, on other grounds, a fairly early date for James seems most probable, we have to ask how the evidence for a 'misunderstood Paulinism' fits in. It has been persuasively argued by D.J. Moo, that the perverted form of Paul's teaching contested in James may be very early rather than very late[28] and there is much to commend this. We know that by the time Paul came to write Romans in AD 57, some aspects of his teaching were already being misrepresented (Rom.3.8) and by that time he had already been preaching the gospel for some years. It is not necessary to assume that Paul was long dead before anyone misunderstood what he taught. 4. The conflict between James and Paul is more apparent than real, because they are addressing different issues, and/or are using the words 'justify' and 'faith' to mean quite different things. If this position is correct James and Paul may each have written without any reference to the other. This is a tempting solution, though there are bad reasons as well as good ones for taking it. If it is adopted largely on the grounds that we must at all costs prevent two parts of the NT from contradicting each other, that is a bad reason. It is essential to attend as carefully as possible to what the texts are actually saying, and to grant them their own individual integrities. If it is true that the conflict between James and Paul is more apparent than real, then this can only be established by careful exegesis. We shall look at this matter in more detail when we come to the relevant part of the letter.

The discussion about whether James and Paul are opposed on the question of what justifies a human being before God has, until recent years, taken it for granted that we are all agreed on what Paul meant by justification by faith and, moreover, that it was at the heart of his understanding of what it means to be a Christian. According to this traditional position Paul's greatest single contribution to Christian self-understanding lies in his decisive rejection of any idea that by keeping 'the law' any human being can earn God's acceptance. Thus, large parts of Galatians and Romans (as well as Ephesians where that is judged to be by Paul) have been interpreted as an attack on the Judaism within which Paul had grown up, with its emphasis on attaining righteousness by keeping the law and performing good deeds. What is sometimes called the 'new perspective' in Pauline studies raises some fundamental questions in this area which need to be considered. Detailed examination of the issues raised by this shift in perspective would be far outside the scope of this commentary, but they cannot be ignored. Our understanding of Paul's attitude to the works of the law and what he meant by justification by faith has inevitable repercussions for our understanding of James.

Although earlier writers (most notably Albert Schweitzer and William Wrede) had, in different ways, questioned the centrality of 'justification by faith' in the thought of Paul,[29] it was really the work of Krister Stendahl in modern times which provided the impetus for a major re-evaluation.[30] Stendahl argued that for too long Western Christianity had read Paul through the eyes of Luther. Luther's central question was 'How may I find a gracious God?' As is well known, he found his answer in Paul's teaching on justification. For him, Paul's rejection of any kind of works-righteousness came as nothing less than a revelation. His long search for personal peace with God was ended when he came to understand what Paul was saying, and his tormented conscience found rest. Luther's experience, and the theology he built upon it, has become the perspective through which Western Christianity (or at least the Protestant part of it) has largely understood Paul. But what if 'How may I find a gracious God?' was *not* the primary question Paul was tackling when he wrote about justification by grace through faith? What if Luther – and perhaps Augustine before him – used Paul's teaching to resolve burning theological issues which were important to them, but which it was not originally designed to meet? In Stendahl's view this is the case. Paul, he thinks, was not so much dealing with a troubled conscience as exploring the nature of Christian discipleship for a Gentile community. Did Paul's converts (especially in Galatia) need to come to Christ through the Jewish law, or did they not? To put the question another way, was it necessary for a Gentile who became a Christian to become a Jew first? If indeed this *is* the principal issue which Paul is concerned to address in Galatians, it does demand some reconsideration of what Paul meant by 'faith alone' as the grounds of salvation.

An even more radical reappraisal of Pauline theology is demanded by the writings of E.P. Sanders. In the space available it is impossible to summarize all his arguments, but some indication needs to be given of their main thrust. Through a detailed examination of the Jewish literature, Sanders has shown that much of the interpretative framework through which NT scholarship has viewed the Judaism of NT times is misleading. The common picture of Judaism as a works religion, concerned to achieve salvation by piling up merit through good deeds, is simply not borne out by the evidence. On the contrary, the Judaism of this period was characterized by what Sanders calls 'covenantal nomism'. He defines it as follows: '. . . the view that one's place in God's plan is established on the basis of the covenant and that the covenant requires as the proper response of man his obedience to its commandments, while providing means of atonement for transgression'.[31] God's choice of Israel is the starting point for such belief, and the law is also seen as God's gift, carrying with it the requirement to obey. The law itself provides for means of atonement, and such atonement results in the maintenance or (where it has been broken) the re-establishment of the covenantal relationship. Judaism did not see obedience as an activity which built up merit in God's sight. Rather, in the literature of the period it is 'universally held to be the behaviour appropriate to being in the covenant, not the means of earning God's grace'.[32] Now if this is so – and nobody has yet shown that Sanders is wrong in his general contention – we need to recognize that something very significant has happened to the traditional picture of what Paul might have meant when he wrote: 'For no human being can be justified in the sight of God by keeping the law' (Rom. 3.20). Assumptions that this is an attack on the Judaism in which he had grown up are demolished once it is recognized that this same Judaism would never have made any such claim.

Sanders' understanding of Paul is equally radical, though his conclusions here command widespread, rather than total acceptance. Broadly, he argues that Paul and the Judaism of his time are, properly understood, in agreement on many things, not least on the relationship between grace and works. Where they differ, and it is a very basic disagreement, is on the total *type* of religion involved. Paul, he judges, thinks in *transfer* terms: righteousness is a matter of participating in Christ, and this is achieved by transferring from the group of those who are perishing to the group of those who are being saved.[33] It can be summed up in this way: 'In Judaism, that is, commitment to the covenant puts one "in", while obedience (righteousness) subsequently keeps one in. In Paul's usage, "be made righteous" ("be justified") is a term indicating getting in, not staying in the body of the saved. Thus when Paul says that one cannot be made righteous by works of law, he means that one cannot, by works of law, "transfer to the body of the saved".'[34] As we might expect, debate on the perspective opened up by Sanders has been vigorous and the literature is immense.[35] It is far beyond the scope of this commentary to engage with these issues, and we do not have to agree with all that Sanders and others are saying, but it is certainly true that in the light of this work some old questions can be approached in fresh ways.

So far as the Epistle of James is concerned, this 'new perspective' suggests that there may be more common ground between James and Paul than has been supposed. Rosemary Fletcher expresses it thus: 'The Lutheran polemic of Jewish and Roman Catholic works and Pauline justification by faith has created a false divide in theology and practice which is not present in James nor in Paul, but only in Luther's interpretation of both.'[36] There is perhaps, a certain irony in this. Whereas in the past exegetes sometimes struggled to accommodate the thought of James to what the mighty Paul was saying, this shift in perspective appears to have brought Paul much closer to James! Most significant however, is that on this assessment *both* writers are seen to draw on a common Jewish heritage. To be sure, they develop it in differing ways and for differing purposes, but both would be able to agree that although obedient Christian living is not the means of earning God's grace, it *is* the behaviour appropriate to those who have received the wisdom which is from above, the Spirit of God (James.3.17; Gal.5.22).

James and Jesus

Nowhere in his Epistle does James directly attribute a saying to Jesus, yet all but the most casual readers notice a number of correspondences between James and some of the sayings attributed to Jesus in the synoptic gospels. This, obviously, calls for some explanation, but it may also help us to place James in its correct setting in the life of the early church. Various scholars have produced different lists of correspondences between James and the synoptic gospels, though some of the texts cited have, it must be admitted, little direct connection.[37] Hunting out parallels is an enjoyable scholarly activity, but it is liable to get out of hand and develop into what Samuel Sandmel once described as 'parallelomania'. We do well to be a little cautious. The importance of *linguistic* parallels (not only with the words of Jesus, but with Hellenistic wisdom literature, Old Testament writings or anything else) does not lie in whether they have a word, or even a cluster of words in common. Such parallels are only really significant when the words or clusters of words are operating in the same way in the two texts. Some parallels can be detected on the basis of close linguistic links, which demands a detailed study of the Greek text.[38] In other cases however, it can be argued that the *thematic* similarities are so strong that the later tradition must have been influenced (conceptually if not verbally) by the earlier one.[39]

Proceeding then on the side of caution, we may accept that at least eleven of the many correspondences which have been suggested exhibit sufficiently close relationships to each other to be considered solid evidence that James knows and uses the sayings of Jesus. The parallels which we propose to accept as likely are these: James 1.2 = Matt. 5.11–12; James 1.5 = Matt. 7.7 (Luke 11.9) and Matt. 21.21–2; James 2.5 = Matt. 5.3,5; James 2.13 = Matt. 5.7; James 2.15–16 = Matt. 25.34–35; James 3.12 = Matt. 7.16; James 3.18 = Matt. 5.9; James 4.10 = Matt. 23.12 (Luke 14.11); James 4.11–12 = Matt. 7.1; James 5.2 = Matt. 6.19; James 5.12 = Matt. 5.34–37.

This is not to say, of course, that some of the other proposed correspondences may not be perfectly valid, but those listed above form the bedrock of the evidence. They provide quite sufficient justification for saying that James knew the Jesus tradition well. In addition to these, it is difficult to deny that at many points in the epistle we are aware of the teaching of Jesus being 'in the air' so to speak. Indeed, it is probably not too much to claim that, 'If there were no Gospels, much would still be known about the teaching of Jesus from the Epistle of James'.[40] Neither can it escape our notice that the overwhelming majority of the likely parallels are between James and the Gospel of Matthew, especially from the Sermon on the Mount. How can this be explained?

It has been suggested that the writer of James possessed a copy of Matthew's Gospel or, more likely, that he was accustomed to hearing it read at the Christian meetings he attended.[41] This hypothesis seems unnecessary, as indeed does any theory which postulates direct use of documents. At this stage of development in early Christianity we are dealing with largely oral traditions of the sayings of Jesus. In the milieu from which the Epistle of James drew its materials the words of Jesus were part of the common consciousness, a living tradition still helping to mould the thinking and awareness of the life of the Christian community.[42] James is clearly a part of the process by which those oral traditions came to be collected and put in writing to emerge eventually in the form of 'gospels', but it has not always been easy to see exactly how it fits into this process. In an important study, P. J. Hartin[43] has investigated the relationship between James and those sayings of Jesus which are to be found particularly in the 'Q' source.[44] From his examination of the wisdom tradition in James and in Q he concludes that 'From a content perspective James is midway between Q and Matthew.' It does not follow that there is a direct line of use of documents, but rather that 'we are dealing with a common thought world in which certain traditions are developed against a common cultural and ideological background.'[45] What we are in fact looking at, when we consider the way in which James uses the sayings of Jesus, is the manner in which the Jesus tradition developed within the early Christian communities. From Hartin's work it appears that Q, James and Matthew lie along the same line of development in the tradition, with James representing an intermediate stage between that of Q and Matthew. This makes good sense, though we need to recognize that it is, in the nature of things, conjectural. What appears soundly established is that James uses the Jesus tradition as it has been handed on in Q, but of course, adapting it in his own way to suit his own context and his own concerns.[46] Is it possible to go further than this? It has been argued that it is not just the number of similarities in thought between Jesus and James which are important, but the actual wording of the sayings of Jesus which has influenced the wording of James.[47] This may be claiming too much. We cannot know for sure the exact wording of any saying of Jesus in the form in which it was known to James and the argument is therefore in great danger of becoming a circular one.

Why James (with one possible exception at 5.12) alludes to the sayings of Jesus in somewhat elliptical fashion rather than quoting them directly, remains something of a mystery. It is widely accepted that within the early church there were 'catechisms' of various kinds for the benefit of new converts, and some have claimed to discern them underlying parts of the NT writings.[48] It is not inherently impossible that some of these may have included what was known of the basic teaching of Jesus in the particular Christian community in which each circulated. If so, it is possible that new Christians memorized such teaching as part of their initiation into the Church. But it remains unclear why allusion should be regarded as more fruitful than direct citation.[49] In this respect we must accept that at present we do not know the answer. In the light of all this, what can be said about a life-setting for the epistle, and therefore a possible date and authorship?

Life-setting, date and authorship

James is, according to one writer, 'one of those apparently timeless documents that could be dated almost anywhere'.[50] Indeed, dates ranging from AD 40 to 130 have been suggested, and very few of these can be dismissed out of hand.[51] However, in the light of recent scholarship we can begin to reduce the options a little. One of the most difficult problems in any study of James is knowing how to account for two elements of the writing which, at first sight, are contrary to each other. On the one hand, there are the markedly Jewish features, pointing strongly to a Palestinian provenance. On the other hand there are many things which point to the world of Hellenistic culture, especially in language and imagery.

The Jewish heritage of the epistle seems clear enough. Nowhere are Jewish practices defended, they are simply assumed.[52] The frequent references to 'the law' by which Christians are to live (1.25; 2.8; 2.12; 4.11–12), however they are to be interpreted, reflect an understanding which draws on and develops OT concepts rather than directly contradicting them. The reference to the Christian gathering as a 'synagogue' (2.2, somewhat obscured in REB by the translation 'meeting'), and the writer's assumption that the readers will know all about Rahab without detailed explanation (2.25) are both significant. He can also refer to 'our father Abraham', which suggests a Jewish Christian writing to Jewish Christians, whereas when Paul does the same to a Christian community at the heart of the Roman Empire he needs to add 'our ancestor by natural descent' (Rom.4.1). Those who hold authority within the Christian community are simply teachers (3.1) or elders (5.14) from which it seems as if the various orders of Christian ministry have not by this stage managed to develop into anything like the formal positions we find in say, I Cor. 12.28, let alone the Pastoral Epistles. It also fits well with the kind of leadership Luke describes in the Jerusalem church at this period (Acts 11.30; 15.2; 16.4; 21.18). A number of scholars have pointed to the significance of the seemingly innocent phrase 'the early and late rains' (5.7), which has been argued to refer to a weather phenomenon typical only of Palestine or Syria. Whilst there are more than a few difficulties in sorting out the social and economic background against which James ought to be read, there are good grounds for arguing that James' treatment of the themes of poverty and wealth, particularly his picture of farmers and hired labourers (5.1–6) and the rich oppressors (2.6–7), fit the Palestine of the period prior to the Fall of Jerusalem in AD 70 better than any other.[53] Further, there is no hint within the epistle that by the time of its writing there had been any major breach between Christianity and Judaism. Although Matthew's Gospel (with which, as we have seen, James has much in common) seems at times to take up an almost self-consciously apologetic position for its own brand of Christian Judaism, there is no such sense in James. There is also an entire absence of themes which might be of special concern to Gentile Christians, such as circumcision or dietary regulations.[54] Arguments from silence are always extremely dangerous, and the evidence is certainly not as unambiguous as some would like it to be. Nevertheless, the strong Jewish and Palestinian strain in James is difficult to deny.

So however, is the evidence of Hellenistic culture, and it is this which has made many hesitate to ascribe it definitely to a Palestinian background and an early date. No direct dependence of James on any one Hellenistic writing has ever been proved, but detailed studies have found strong links with a number of them. In some cases these amount to little more than occasional verbal agreements. In other cases it has been claimed that by an examination of 'consistent clusters and patterns' of words, *topoi* (subjects which are the commonplaces of Greek rhetorical writing) can be traced in James as clearly as in Hellenistic moral philosophy.[55] Certainly the writer often shows considerable ease in employing the literary idioms and conventions of Greek thought (see the commentary on 1.23–25), though not always (see the commentary on 3.5–12). It may reasonably be asked whether a Palestinian Jewish Christian could have written in this way. Then again, there is the problem of the language of the epistle. A discussion of the writer's Greek style and the quality of his writing would be quite out of place in a commentary like this, but we may briefly note the judgements of the experts. The most exhaustive examination of the grammar and style of the epistle remains that of J.B. Mayor,[56] even though it is now dated in some respects. With some qualifications Mayor's judgement is generally agreed to hold good: 'I should be inclined to rate the Greek of this Epistle as approaching more nearly the standard of classical purity than that of any other book of the N.T. with the exception perhaps of the Epistle to the Hebrews.'[57] It may reasonably be asked how a Palestinian Jewish Christian could possibly write an epistle in excellent Greek when his everyday language was Aramaic.

The need to decide whether James (or any other writing) is

'Palestinian' or 'Hellenistic' only arises when the two are sharply distinguished, as was once thought to be the case. The general assumption used to be that Palestinian Judaism and Hellenistic Judaism were two worlds with no common meeting point. This view now requires considerable modification. Certainly any picture of 'Galilean peasants' of complete cultural insularity and with little education is wholly false. Within the NT itself there are strong hints of a multi-cultural society. According to John 19.19–20 (and some texts of Luke 23.28) Pontius Pilate caused the inscription on the cross of Jesus to be written in Hebrew, Latin and Greek. There appears to have been nothing unusual about such polyglot inscriptions, but there is equally no point in them unless they serve a purpose (public notices in several languages can often be met with in Switzerland or Finland, but only rarely in England or France). In Acts 6.1 the reader is introduced, without prior preparation, to 'Hellenists' and 'Hebrews'[58] already present within the earliest group of believers in Jerusalem itself. The term 'Hellenists' occurs in this verse for the first time in Greek literature, and it refers to Jewish Christians whose mother tongue, or only tongue, was Greek.[59] It is apparent from Acts 6.9 that there existed at least one Greek-speaking synagogue in Jerusalem at this stage. It is becoming increasingly clear that these groups did not exist in isolation from one another, but that 'Hellenistic' Judaism was a part of Palestinian life and culture.[60] Some of the most important advances in biblical scholarship in recent decades enable us to understand that Hellenistic influences played a much larger part in Palestinian life than was once supposed, and that such influences were by no means confined to the wealthy or upper classes. It is true that there were groups who strongly resisted any non-Jewish cultural influences, especially where it was thought that these compromised the observance of Israel's historic faith, but in general terms it may be said that Palestine was quite well integrated into the life of the Hellenistic world, at an economic (Greek was the language of commerce) and administrative level, as well as the cultural one.[61] In the light of these considerations it is not surprising after all, that a Palestinian Christian could show considerable familiarity with the commonplaces of Greek thought, and skill in using them.

Even so, it may still be asked whether such a person could be capable of writing such good Greek as we find in James. J. N. Sevenster has investigated this particular aspect with great thoroughness, using the Epistle of James as a test-case. In the light of new discoveries and advances in biblical scholarship he concludes: 'It has now been clearly demonstrated that a knowledge of Greek was in no way restricted to the upper circles, which were permeated with Hellenistic culture, but was to be found in all circles of Jewish society, and certainly in places bordering on regions where much Greek was spoken, e.g. Galilee.'[62] With specific reference to James he writes: 'in view of all the data made available in the past decades the possibility can no longer be precluded that a Palestinian Jewish Christian of the first century AD wrote an epistle in good Greek.'[63]

Given a possible, even probable setting for James in the life of the Palestinian Christian communities, can we begin to settle on a date when the epistle might have been written? This is not easy, but there are some pointers. If Patrick Hartin's work on how the author of James receives and uses the tradition of the sayings of Jesus[64] stands scrutiny, as it seems to do, then it is very difficult to date James before about AD 55 on those grounds alone. In any case it can be argued that some of the social background reflected in the epistle fits better after AD 55 than earlier. Many, though not all, of the situations addressed in the epistle (which we have already argued reflect at least as much the circumstances of its place of writing as those of its recipients) would have lost their force after the Fall of Jerusalem in AD 70. Perhaps most persuasive of all for a relatively early date, is the teaching on judgement and the coming of the Lord to bring the present world order to an end. In 5.7–9 the readers are counselled to be patient 'until the Lord comes' which, they are assured, 'is near'. Moreover, 'at the door stands the Judge.' This, taken with those passages which point to the transitoriness of life, the possession of the kingdom by those who are rich in faith and love God and the judgement on those who are rich and oppressive (1.10–11; 2.5; 4.14–15; 5.2–3), indicates that James expected the present unjust world order to end at a very early date with the coming of the Lord. This, as we know, was a keen expectation amongst the first generation of Christians. It is prominent, for example, in some of Paul's earlier letters, but was gradually toned down as it became evident that the expectation was mistaken and that the Lord was not going to return within the lifetime of the first Christian believers. James has a primitive doctrine of the end (eschatology), and this points strongly to an early date. We would be wise to look then, for a date before 70, but how much before? The common picture of a Jewish nation in revolt against Roman rule continuously from the beginning of the

Christian era, along with intense activity from Jewish nationalist groups (such as the Zealots) may need some qualification, but Jewish nationalist activity certainly intensified in the 40s and 50s, prior to the war starting in 66. There are hints in James both of the increasing class warfare which this involved, and of the temptation to grasp at material security[65] and possibly of the temptation to become involved in the armed struggle itself (see the commentary on 4.1–4). The picture of what happened to the Christian church in Jerusalem during that period is somewhat confused. The early church historian Eusebius tells us that in the period immediately prior to 66 the Jerusalem church received a revelation telling them to flee and settle in the city of Pella, one of the cities of the Decapolis. Some did flee, but probably to the less populous parts of the Transjordan, whilst others remained in Jerusalem.[66] Whatever we make of this (and there are many uncertainties), it is difficult to believe that James reflects a situation which obtained once the first Jewish Revolt was fully under way, whilst it is entirely consistent with the situation leading up to that revolt. We therefore conclude that a date somewhere between 55 and 66 is the most likely, though nothing in the way of certainty can be attained.

As to who wrote the Epistle of James, that is even more difficult. The document claims to be by James (1.1), and there is only one James who need be seriously considered; that is James the brother of Jesus, who became a leader of the church in Jerusalem and who is usually known as 'James the Just'. James died in 62, so if he wrote the epistle himself (with or without help from someone else) it must obviously be dated before then. This, as we have seen, is not impossible. There is a marked contrast between the role of the brothers of Jesus in the gospels, and in the post-resurrection history of the early church. In the gospel narratives they are depicted as failing to understand the mission in which Jesus was engaged (Mark 3.31–34; Matt. 12.46–49; Luke 8.19–21 and, somewhat differently, John 7.3–11). Though James is not specifically named in those passages he was doubtless included. It is from Mark 6.3 (Matt. 13.55) that we learn specifically about the relationship. Yet by the time of Acts 1.14 the brothers of Jesus were with Mary their mother, a number of the disciples and a group of women, engaged in constant prayer. By the time the narrative of Acts reaches 12.17 James is important enough to be named separately from the other members of the church, and is in a clear position of leadership. It is not without significance that the instruction of the risen Jesus, as recorded in two otherwise unconnected traditions was to 'take word to my brothers' (Matt.28.10; John 20.17). Whilst that may mean 'to my disciples', it can equally well be argued that it means the natural brothers of Jesus,[67] whose presence with the disciples in Acts 1.14 does require some explanation. We may note too, that Matt.28.10 contains the promise of a resurrection appearance, and this could be equally well fulfilled by the appearance to James which Paul tells us about (I Cor.15.7) as by any of the resurrection appearances to the disciples. Be that as it may, James seems to have become an undisputed leader in the Jerusalem church at quite an early date, not necessarily just because he was a relation of Jesus.[68] There are somewhat complicated questions about his relationships with Paul in particular, and his role in the 'Council of Jerusalem' (Acts 15.1–36) but those are not our direct concern here. The Jewish historian Josephus tells us that James was stoned to death on a charge of 'breaking the law', although it is far from clear exactly what is meant by that phrase: it can hardly refer to the law of Moses, but neither do charges of sedition against the Roman authorities seem very likely from what we otherwise know of James. Although Josephus' writings have been subject to much Christian interpolation, his sober, even bald account of the death of James[69] can unquestionably be accepted. Various later accounts, including the one by the Palestinian Christian Hegesippus[70] (written around AD 170) are another matter, and cannot be relied upon.[71]

Could James the Just, brother of Jesus, have written the Epistle of James as we now have it? It has been noted that the opening words 'From James' seem to have a ring of authority about them, as if the writer is so well-known as to have no need to explain who he is. But this hardly settles the issue: II Peter begins in similarly confident fashion, but that document is most unlikely to be from the pen of Simon Peter. The tradition of pseudonymous writing (compositions issued under the the name of a revered teacher, whose memory was thereby honoured) was quite common in the ancient world, although there is some controversy about how widely accepted a practice it was within the Christian community. But if the document is pseudonymous this would hardly be possible within the lifetime of James the Just. Pseudonymity is only a contender if the epistle was written long after his death which, as we have seen, is unlikely. The possibility of James the Just being the author is inevitably affected by our willingness or otherwise to accept that the son of a Galilean carpenter could have acquired sufficiently good Greek to write it.

Some scholars judge that his position of leadership in the Jerusalem church would have impelled him to acquire such skills in order to communicate effectively with his constituency, whilst others find that an implausible hypothesis. Whilst it is not impossible that James the Just could have acquired the linguistic skills necessary to write the letter, it is perhaps more doubtful that he could have become as totally at ease with the imagery and conventions as our author appears to be. It is not inconceivable that the epistle could have been compiled from his addresses to the church and put into good Greek by someone else. It would have been quite natural for an educated Christian Jew who lived outside Palestine, but who travelled regularly to Jerusalem and visited the mother church there to undertake such a task. This could have been done with James' approval, as a way of communicating with the Jewish Christian communities outside Palestine, or shortly after his death as a means of preserving the distinctive style and flavour of his teaching. Indeed, it may be that here and there in the letter we can detect the hand of such an editor, in the relatively sudden changes of subject, and particularly in 5.12–19, where the various topics seem to have been brought together because they needed to be included somewhere, rather than because they form any very logical sequence. R.P. Martin argues that the epistle as we now have it is the work of an editor later than James, but working on material which originated from him.[72] A theory of editorial revision certainly helps to account for many of the Hellenistic idioms and literary flourishes, and a two-stage theory of composition also enables us to recover the redactional unity of the text.[73] However, Martin is somewhat too confident that we can discover the precise readership for whom the text was so edited. A perfect solution to the problem of the authorship of the Epistle of James does not exist. The theory of a Hellenistic Jew, who acted as editor in order to preserve and communicate material originating from James the Just, within his lifetime or very shortly after his death, accounts for more difficulties than most

The structure of the Epistle of James

The view of Dibelius, formulated in the 1920s, that 'large portions of James reveal no continuity in thought whatsoever',[74] remained critical orthodoxy for many years. The pendulum of critical judgement has recently swung in quite the opposite direction – arguably too much so. One scholar has discerned eight homiletic-didactic discourses, each grouped round what he describes as a 'gnomic saying'.[75] Another writer makes the novel suggestion that James was judged to be about as much as a congregation could digest at one sitting, and that it is divided into 'two balanced, coherent, and yet, within proper limits, almost self-sufficient instalments' within which there are thirteen units.[76] In his commentary, J. B. Adamson suggests that the opening formula is followed by eight distinct sections forming a kind of rondo,[77] and P. H. Davids offers five major sections enclosing fourteen sub-sections.[78] P. J. Hartin discerns four main sections, with seventeen sub-sections.[79] The difficulty is that no two of these scholars agree either on the number of main or sub-sections into which the epistle should be divided nor, by and large, where any of them begin or end, much less on the titles which should be given to them.

There is a danger that producing a structure in advance for any NT letter will shape, or even determine, the course of the interpretation, and there is much to be said for not working to any predetermined plan. We certainly do not share the view that the Epistle of James is shapeless or devoid of any continuity or structure, but we are equally wary about tightly drawn schemes which ignore some of the diversity to be found within it. Some themes run like threads through the cloth of the epistle, yet there are gaps, and some abrupt introduction of new material. The commentary which follows will therefore content itself with using the headings introduced by the editors of the Revised English Bible. They are not perfect, but they are a good starting point.

What matters most, is that we catch something of the fervour and dynamism with which James bears witness to the need to 'act on the message' (1.22) which we have received and not to deceive ourselves by thinking that listening is sufficient. When James is heard in that way it will prove as relevant at the close of the twentieth century as it did to those who first heard it – and as uncomfortable!

COMMENTARY

Address and greeting
1.1

In the contemporary Western world letters usually begin with the name of the person to whom they are addressed, and are signed by the writer at their conclusion. In Hellenistic letters it was more usual to begin by identifying the person in whose name the document was being sent, together with the addressees. This procedure is followed here. It does not of itself establish that the document is a letter, nor that the writer is James the Just (see the Introduction: 'Life-Setting, Date and Authorship' for a discussion of both these points). It is natural to ask why, if the writer *is* James the brother of Jesus, he does not say so, since at the very least it might be thought that this would add authority to what he teaches. The author's natural modesty has sometimes been suggested as the reason for this, in the same way in which the disciple John is never named in the Gospel which bears his name, but always referred to as 'the disciple whom Jesus loved'. A better reason might be that, even if there is a close family relationship, James recognizes that this alone is not a basis for authority in the church.[1] James has such authority as a leader of the church in Jerusalem, but it comes from his eventual faith in Jesus as more than his natural brother, a faith which was confirmed and strengthened by the appearance of the risen Lord to him personally (I Cor. 15.7). The gospel traditions record Jesus as teaching that in the kingdom of God preparedness to do the will of God matters infinitely more than blood-ties (Mark 3.35). If the material of this letter does go back to the brother of Jesus, who would know that teaching better than he? Be that as it may, he is here content to describe himself as *servant* (Gk.*doulos*), a word which literally means 'slave', and is so used for example, in Eph. 6.5–9, when the relationship between slaves and their owners, and of both to God, is under discussion. In the opening formula of a letter 'servant' is undoubtedly the right translation. We should not though, take it as merely a stock phrase (perhaps akin to the conventional ending 'Your obedient servant' in certain traditions of English letter-writing). It reflects the writer's awareness of unworthiness to bear the message and also something of the necessity of so doing. Paul sometimes uses this description of himself (Rom.1.1; Phil.1.1), but more often calls himself an 'apostle' (I Cor.1.1; II Cor.1.1; Gal.1.1; Col.1.1), a title which James does not claim (though see Gal.1.19). He writes then, as a servant of *God and the Lord Jesus Christ*. This is a most unusual phrase, parallelled in the NT, and then only slightly, by Tit.1.1. 'Servant of God' is familiar to us from the Old Testament where it describes outstanding religious leaders (such as Moses, Deut.34.5); 'Servant of Christ Jesus' is Paul's phrase. It is on the whole more likely that James is here using 'Christ' to mean 'Messiah' than as the proper name it later became. By using the two phrases in conjunction with each other he may be indicating what it means to a monotheistic Jew to come to terms with the recognition that the one true God is now best known and understood through the Christ. Much of what follows in the epistle will be concerned with how the ability to live well in God's world can be shaped by the coming of Jesus as well as by the inherited traditions of Judaism.

James sends his *greetings* (a conventional way of opening a letter) to the *twelve tribes dispersed throughout the world*. The Greek word translated *dispersed* is *diaspora*, which is still used today to refer to Jews who live outside the state of Israel. What is usually termed the 'exile' began with those Jews who were taken from Judah to Babylon by Nebuchadnezzar in 598 BC, and who were later joined by others after 587 BC. Although some returned after 538 BC with the Persian conquest of Babylon, many did not, but continued to live on in exile, to discover, often painfully, in what ways it was possible to sing the Lord's song in a foreign land (Ps.137.4). The way in which diaspora Judaism developed out of the exile is not altogether clear to us, but by NT times there were well-established Jewish communities in many cities throughout the Roman empire and beyond. They retained important links with their homeland (see Acts 2.5) though the task of coming to terms with the idea that one could be a good Jew and yet live outside the land God had given, involved the development of new spiritual and theological resources.[2] The plain and literal meaning of the epistle's address is therefore to fellow Jews living outside Palestine. Christian Jews must be meant, since the epistle largely deals with the concerns of Christians and there are few signs that it is intended as an evangelistic writing. However, this is not absolutely certain: I Peter was almost certainly written to either a Gentile or a mixed Jewish and Gentile community of Christians, and that letter is addressed to those of the 'diaspora' (REB, 'the scattered people of God now living as aliens'). I Peter may be an example of the way in which Christians gradually began to take over the names and titles formerly applied to Israel, though that process was more patchy than has sometimes been supposed.[3] It is unlikely that James already thinks of the Christian church as the 'new Israel'[4] and better to take the epistle as written to Christian Jews who, although they may have visited Jerusalem and the mother church, were living out their Christian lives amongst Jewish communities outside Palestine. The *twelve tribes* had, of course, long ago ceased to exist as such, but the phrase became symbolic of the time when God's kingdom would come in all its fullness (cp. Matt.19.28).

Faith under trial

1.2–27

1.2 *My friends* is the REB's laudable attempt to translate the Greek into gender-neutral language, but it risks obscuring James' characteristic address to his readers, which is 'brothers' (Gk.*adelphoi*). We might appropriately translate it today as 'My brothers and sisters' (NRSV). James uses this word here and a further seventeen times in the epistle (sometimes 'brothers', but also as here 'my brothers', and on three occasions 'my dear brothers'), an unusually high number of occurrences in so short a document.[1] Its frequent use by Christian writers cannot easily be ascribed to any background in the OT, although the concept may be implicit in such practices as the remission of debts and the forbidding of usury to fellow Hebrews.[2] It is however, a particularly appropriate term within the Christian community. We may recall Paul's description of Jesus as the 'eldest among a large family of brothers' (Rom.8.29) and find there the theological justification for regarding the community of believers in such a way. In James this term is often used in the context of moral exhortation and encouragement. We can hear the authentic voice of deep pastoral concern, expressed so well by the Puritan Richard Baxter many centuries later: 'When the people see that you unfeignedly love them, they will hear anything and bear anything and follow you the more easily'.[3] And indeed, the call to bear anything is what comes next. James tells his readers that when they find themselves facing *all sorts of trials* they must count themselves *supremely happy*. What sorts of trials might these be, and why should anyone undergoing them respond in such a way (literally: 'count it all joy') when most people would regard it as a natural human reaction to avoid as much testing and affliction as possible? The possibility cannot be excluded that in *trials* James includes such troubles as illness (5.13, though a different word is used), but it is far more likely that here he refers more to the kinds of trials which might come their way specifically on account of the faith which they profess (2.6–7) or even those which make it difficult to live faithfully by the gospel when there are blatant shortcomings and divisions within the Christian fellowship, defects which may themselves be viewed as the work of evil (3.13–4.12, esp.3.15, 4.4). Trials which take the form of persecutions are perhaps the most likely, since the notion of having *to face* them suggests that they largely come from outside the community. Of course, there is more than one kind or degree of persecution. Attempts on the part of those in authority to silence Christian preaching by imprisonment, physical ill-treatment and execution (whether that recorded in the Acts of the Apostles, those emerging from the archives of the former Soviet Union or from any from the centuries in between) form only one kind of persecution, if the most dramatic. Such persecution often only serves to strengthen the persecuted; 'The blood of the martyrs is the seed of the church' as Tertullian rightly observed. Other kinds of persecution such as continual harassment, economic pressures and social or peer-group disapproval, though less obvious, may be harder to counter, subtly lowering resistance and inviting compromise. These kinds of trials, rather than outright martyrdom, seem to be envisaged in this epistle.

1.3   Why should those who face trials react in the way James recommends? Knowing that *such testing of your faith makes for strength to endure* is a part, though only a part, of the answer. It is true that in Jewish spirituality there was a tradition of looking to those whose faith was specially tested and who either endured it successfully (like Abraham and Job) or failed dreadfully (like the Israelites in their wilderness journeyings). Up to this point, James' meaning might indeed be this. But in the case of Abraham and Job, such testing either came from, or was specially permitted by, God (Gen.22; Job 1.6–12, 2.1–6), and James will use the example of Abraham at least, for a rather different purpose (2.23–24). In any case, the Jewish tradition thought of such testing as educative: that is to say, by undergoing such tests people learned how strong their faith really was, but James views them somewhat differently. The endurance of tests and trials is not an end in itself, however helpful it might be in the field of spiritual self-knowledge; rather it is connected with what will happen in the future.[4] Those who undergo such *testing* know that it has an end result, which is *strength to endure*. Outside James, the word translated *testing* (*dokimion*) only comes once more in the NT, at I Peter 1.7 where REB describes it as a faith which 'stands the test'. Those who find the background of this idea in the LXX,[5] where the two occurrences of *dokimion* both refer to the process whereby precious metals are refined by fire, are probably right. Such difficulties and trials are not pointless, even though they may seem so at the time, nor do they decide whether a person has any faith (that is assumed), nor do they merely increase the believer's self-awareness. On the contrary, they refine the faith which is already there, so giving it the strength to endure what is still to come, and to do so to the end. This is why the readers have been told to reckon themselves *supremely happy* (v.2), though a quality of real and deep joy is meant, not a superficial happiness. In looking to the end result of such a process (a thought which is developed in the next verse) and in stressing the joy, James seems to be echoing some of the teaching of the Sermon on the Mount. It is reminiscent in particular of Matt.5.11–12: 'Blessed are you, when you suffer insults and persecution and calumnies of every kind for my sake. Exult and be glad, for you have a rich reward in heaven; in the same way they persecuted the prophets before you.' The verbal parallels are not close, but the thought is, particularly in its stress on the final benefit.

1.4   Those whose faith is refined in the way James has described, have both something to do and something to look forward to. What they have to do is to allow this endurance to *perfect its work* in them, or in Mayor's memorable translation: 'Let it have its full effect.'[6] What they may then hope for is that they may *become perfected*, which almost inevitably recalls Matt. 5.48 where the command to 'be perfect' is in imitation of God: 'as your heavenly Father is perfect' (NIV). This perfection is of Christian character as a whole rather than any one specific quality. Despite the many difficulties in which Christians have found themselves when trying to speak of Christian perfection[7] it remains important not only as goal and aspiration, but as here in James, as the final outworking of a faith which endures. Believers may also look forward to becoming *sound throughout* (better perhaps 'fully developed', NJB) which is about wholeness and completion of character, and *lacking in nothing* which, whilst it recalls Jesus' word to the rich young man who had kept all the commandments, 'One thing you lack'[8] here refers to the fullness of the Christian's future hope. Amy Carmichael (who knew her own share of trials and testing, when circumstances frustrated her clear sense of vocation) wrote: 'It is not really what we go through that

8

matters, it is what we go under that breaks us. We can bear anything if only we are kept inwardly victorious.'[9] How believers may be kept 'inwardly victorious' is largely the subject of the next few verses.

1.5   If the aim of the fully formed Christian character is to be 'lacking in nothing' (v.4), then an awareness that one might lack *wisdom* is a serious matter. James specifically discusses wisdom here, and in 3.13–18, and it has been suggested that the idea is also implicit in 1.16–18. It is clearly an important theme of the epistle and has a background in the OT and in the wider literature of Judaism, without which it cannot be properly appreciated. The archetypal 'wise man' of the canonical OT writings is Solomon. The tradition relates that shortly after his accession to the throne God appeared to him and asked, 'What shall I give you?' In response, Solomon requested 'wisdom and knowledge' and this pleased God who granted him not only what he had requested, but also those things which he had not asked for, wealth, possessions and glory unmatched by any other monarch (I Kings 3.5–15; II Chron. 1.7–12). The story of the two prostitutes with one living baby follows immediately in the Kings narrative (I Kings 3.16–27) as a vivid illustration not only that Solomon had been granted the wisdom he had asked for, but of the nature of that wisdom. It was essentially practical, a quality which would show itself in just governing, the distinguishing of truth from falsehood and good from evil. It has been described as a quality of understanding, a feeling for the truth.[10] At the same time, it was more than simple human shrewdness and, as the story clearly demonstrates, it was regarded as a gift from God, not something which Solomon could have acquired for himself. In due course a 'wisdom literature' appeared within Judaism (Proverbs, Ecclesiastes, just a few of the Psalms and, more arguably, Job in the canonical OT; The Wisdom of Solomon and Ecclesiasticus in the Apocrypha). The name of Solomon was often associated with this, doubtless because he was said to have composed over six thousand proverbs and songs (I Kings 4.32). These wisdom writings focus on practical aspects of living faithfully in God's world yet continue to stress that wisdom is a gift of God. Indeed, in those passages where wisdom is personified as 'Lady Wisdom' (Prov. 3.15–20; 8.1–9.6) it is possible to see how wisdom came to be regarded as both the rules of wise and good living which the sages wished to commend, and as a figure associated with God from the beginning. Lady Wisdom therefore 'comes to bear two birthmarks: the mark of human wisdom learned through experience, and the mark of the divine wisdom of God, revealed by God through his creation'.[11] In the later literature wisdom is sometimes identified with the law of Moses: 'I took root among the people whom the Lord had honoured by choosing them to be his own portion . . . All this is the book of the covenant of God Most High, the law laid on us by Moses, a possession for the assemblies of Jacob' (Ecclus. 24.12,23). At other times wisdom is described in terms almost indistinguishable from the Spirit of God: 'I was taught by wisdom, by her whose skill made all things. In wisdom there is a spirit intelligent and holy, unique in its kind yet made up of many parts, subtle, free-moving, lucid, spotless, clear, neither harmed nor harming, loving what is good, eager, unhampered, beneficent, kindly towards mortals, steadfast, unerring, untouched by care, all-powerful, all-surveying, and permeating every intelligent, pure, and most subtle spirit' (Wisd. 7.22–3). Whilst it is an exaggeration to describe Jesus as a 'wisdom teacher', there are noteworthy passages in which his teaching is presented almost within this wisdom tradition, most obviously when he contrasted the contemporary reception of his teaching with the Queen of Sheba's response to the wisdom of Solomon (Matt.12.42; Luke 11.31, see also Matt.11.19; 23.34). Other NT writers do not hesitate to describe Jesus as the 'wisdom of God' (I Cor.1.24) and the preaching of the gospel as instruction in 'all the ways of wisdom' (Col.1.28). James stands firmly within this tradition of 'Christian wisdom'[12] as it built upon its Jewish foundations. Those who lack wisdom, lack the ability to conduct their lives in the way God requires and to walk in the way which has now been shown through Christ. The lack of wisdom is therefore a serious matter, and someone in this position should *ask God and it will be given him, for God is a generous giver*. James here echoes the teaching of Jesus about the importance of asking and its result: 'Ask, and you will receive; seek, and you will find. . . . for everyone who asks receives' (Matt.7.7–8; Luke 11.9–10), and stresses the reason for this. It is in the nature and character of God to be responsive to those who ask, almost part of the definition of what it means for us to call God a 'heavenly Father' (Matt.7.11; Luke 11.13). Yet there is, it seems, a condition to be attached.

1.6 The one who prays for wisdom must *ask in faith, with never a doubt in his mind*, which is the other side of the coin from the willingness of God to give. The difficult story of Jesus and the fig tree which withered (Mark 11.22–25; Matt.21.18–22) gave rise to teaching on prayer which seems closely paralleled here. In both places the emphasis is on asking without doubting, but there are differences too. In the gospel accounts the stress is on the power of faith which, if it is strong enough, can even (metaphorically speaking of course) move mountains. The same graphic image is found in Matt.17.20, where Jesus addresses the disciples following the expulsion of a demon from an epileptic boy, but only in the fig tree story does Jesus add: 'Whatever you pray for in faith you will receive' (Matt.21.22). In James, faith has certainly been under discussion, particularly in terms of its being tested and tried, but there is no illustration, startling or otherwise, as there is in the gospels, of the power of faith. It is simply that faith is required when the prayer for wisdom is made. In view of the description of the doubting person as *like a wave of the sea tossed hither and thither by the wind*, it is probable that the kind of faith James envisages here is *more* than a confidence that the request will be granted, important though that is. The doubter, in this context, is one whose fundamental allegiance wavers.[13] Sincerely to want to follow in the way of God's wisdom is to desire something which directs the whole of a person's life and conduct. To ask for this triflingly or uncertainly means that the one who prays is not yet ready, or fully able, to receive what is being asked for. This passage does not, of course, contain a full Christian theology of prayer. There are many times when Christians pray, but hardly know what they should pray for, in which situation they can rely on the aid of the Spirit (Rom.8.26), and the request 'help my unbelief' (Mark 9.24) met with a favourable response from Jesus. James is here concerned with a person's basic intention, and only when that intention is to walk in the way of wisdom – however faltering the actual accomplishment may be – can the prayer be said to be offered *with never a doubt*.

1.7   The person who prays, but with no real intention of allowing his or her way of life to be affected, has already effectively prevented God from answering the prayer! That is why anyone praying in such a way cannot reasonably expect to *receive anything from the Lord*. If this point is not understood – and James clearly envisages people who do not understand it – it is because the whole nature of prayer as an orientation of human life to God's wisdom has not been grasped. Prayer is not so much words we say, or even requests we make (though James will deal later with those), as the attitude with which we approach life; in this case the willingness to receive and live by the wisdom of God.

1.8 The *doubter* (who is still being described here), is *always in two minds and unstable in all he does*. James uses a rare Greek word (*dipsuchos*), which never occurs in the LXX, nor in previous literature, though it quickly became current amongst early Christian writers, and he uses it again at 4.8 in much the same way.[14] P.H. Davids is right to look for its background in OT theology,[15] rather than its use in such writings as The Shepherd of Hermas and the First and Second Epistles of Clement of Rome[16] which on our reckoning are later than James and develop the term differently. It is related to the idea that loving God with all of one's heart and soul and strength is a primary requirement of those who confess the faith of Israel, well illustrated by the famous *Shema* (Deut.6.5). Following God's way involves avoiding the hypocrisy and lies of those who 'talk with smooth words, but with duplicity in their hearts' (Ps.12.2). This double hearted/mindedness is also condemned in the wisdom literature, especially in Ecclesiasticus: 'Do not disregard the fear of the Lord, or approach him without sincerity. Do not act a part before the eyes of the world' (Ecclus.1.28–29b); and 'Woe to faint hearts and nerveless hands and to the sinner who leads a double life!' (Ecclus 2.12). Amongst the Covenanters of Qumran there was a notion of conflict between the spirit of truth and the spirit of perversion, a conflict taking place within the hearts of human beings. For the people of Qumran, retaining hold of evil things (or allowing them to retain hold on you) whilst at the same time attempting to serve God or pretending to do so, was double hearted/mindedness.[17] So then, even if the origins of the term are a touch obscure, what James means by it here is clear enough. Such doubters as he has been describing in vv.6–7, are vacillating, unable to make up their minds whether they really do want to serve God or whether they do not. There might be all sorts of reasons for such a situation, though perhaps the chief one is nearly always an unwillingness to face the cost of becoming single-minded in living by the values of God's kingdom. One commentator not inappropriately cites St Augustine's well-known youthful prayer as an example: 'O Lord, grant me chastity, but not yet.'[18] Such a person is almost by definition *unstable in all he does*, not to be wholly trusted nor relied upon, because wholeness of personality and purpose is lacking. The opposite of this (though there is no evidence that James has it directly in mind here) is surely the Beatitude 'Blessed are those whose hearts are pure; they shall see God' (Matt.5.8). That Beatitude describes 'those whose motives are absolutely unmixed, whose minds are utterly sincere, who are completely and totally single-minded'.[19]

1.9 James now introduces a completely new topic. *The church member* (literally, 'brother') *in humble circumstances* is now the focus of attention. It seems clear from this epistle that in the Christian communities James knew there were both poor and wealthy members (see the commentary on 1.10, 2.15–16). This was certainly the case with the church in Jerusalem in its earliest days, for the experiment in communal sharing (Acts 4.32–37) was only possible because some people possessed lands and properties which could be sold and the proceeds shared with the needy. How far that process drained the resources of the membership of the church at that time, making them less able to survive in difficult circumstances, is uncertain, although we do know that Paul needed to organize a collection amongst his Gentile converts for the Jerusalem church in response to a direct request he had received from the leaders of that church to 'keep in mind the poor' (Gal.2.10a). The date of that request is difficult to determine, though AD 46 and 49 are both possibilities. When the leaders of the Jerusalem church made that request they may have had in mind the poorer members of the congregation, or they may have been indicating that the church as a whole had by that time become poverty-stricken.[20] If the latter, circumstances had evidently improved somewhat by the time this epistle was written. It is evident that the Christian message made a special appeal to ordinary people, who had, after all, listened eagerly to Jesus (Mark 12.37). Both amongst Jewish and Gentile converts there were many people *in humble circumstances.* Servants were found in some congregations (I Peter 2.18), slaves and their masters in others (Eph. 6.5,9). In the Corinthian church some of the poorer members had insufficient to eat and drink, while others clearly had more than was good for them (I Cor. 11.20–22). So too in James; the congregation is a socially mixed one. So far as the poor members are concerned, they should take *pride in being exalted.* This is a surprising assertion, because taking pride, or boasting, usually has negative associations in the NT and Christian spirituality in general, but also because it is not immediately obvious what it means to speak of such a person being *exalted.* The first difficulty is not a real one. There is such a thing as a proper pride, and it is encountered most often when its object is something for which the 'boaster' claims no credit. For example, if parents 'take pride' in their children's good character (provided they do not ascribe it entirely to parental influence) that is not usually regarded as morally reprehensible. The supreme NT example is that of Paul, determined to 'boast' of nothing except the cross of Christ for which, self-evidently, he could claim no credit at all (Gal. 6.14). In understanding what it means for the humble church member to be *exalted*, it is necessary to reflect on the nature of the gospel which such a person had received. Within the ministry of Jesus himself, we see the lowly becoming exalted as they hear his teaching, recognize the unconditional love of God for them, and are thereby set free to contemplate a new world of life and action.[21] That process continued and deepened as people responded to the early Christian preaching. James is speaking here of the spiritual enrichment which comes to those who know themselves to belong to Christ. As C. L. Mitton expresses it: 'Outwardly he may still be a slave, or a poorly paid servant, little valued by those who use his labour, and hardly noticed by his fellow-servants; but he now knows himself to be a child of God, a joint heir with Christ, the Lord's freedman.'[22] Further, this humble member is also a 'brother', with all that properly implies in terms of equality within the life of the church. It is a fact of Christian history that revival movements have often attracted considerable numbers of the poor and marginalized, and have given dignity and worth to their lives. It is also a fact of Christian history that the church has all too often imported social distinctions into the life of the congregation, thereby denying what James is here at such pains to affirm: the person in *humble circumstances* has already been *exalted* by his or her salvation in Christ and incorporation into the Christian community.

1.10   Another aspect of the same truth is now stressed: *the wealthy member must find his pride in being brought low*. James does not actually use the word 'brother' again of the rich person; 'but the one who is rich' (NIV) renders the Greek more literally. It is quite difficult to decide whether the wealthy person *is* a church member, or whether James has in view a poor church member and a wealthy non-Christian. In favour of the former view is the the fact that the word *wealthy* looks as if it ought to balance *humble* in the previous verse. In favour of the latter view is the difficulty of supposing that James envisages a member of the Christian congregation who, for no other reason than that he happens to be wealthy, will, as the next verse makes plain, have no future beyond death. A number of solutions have been proffered, but none is entirely satisfactory. It is best to see a single thought running through vv.9 and 10, and to see v.11 as an example of those rather loose connections of thought sometimes met with in this writing. In v.10 James probably does refer to a wealthy Christian. Just as the poorer Christian can take great pride and encouragement in the new status which has come with salvation in Christ, so the wealthier Christian must take pride in exactly the same thing, and for the same reason. Indeed, he has nothing else in which he *can* take pride. If it is true that a human life is given dignity, worth and true status only by what a person is in the sight of God, then that is true for all. The wealthy Christian will also recognize that, and will properly *find his pride* in the way in which all his riches (which bring status and worth in a world that does not know the way of Christian wisdom) count for nothing in the sight of God or his fellow Christians.[23] That is indeed to be *brought low* as others see it, but it is a source of pride for those who know the love of God. At this point James' train of thought becomes diverted, for he has mentioned the rich, and it is a favourite topic (2.1–7; 4.13–5.6) for which is reserved some of the strongest language in the epistle. It has the effect of producing more general reflections on the fate of the rich, not directly connected with the future of the rich Christian who has just been mentioned. *The rich man will disappear like a wild flower* is probably a proverbial saying, though it is more than a little reminiscent of Ps. 103.15: 'The days of a mortal are as grass; he blossoms like a wild flower in the meadow', and also of Isa. 40.6–7, though both those passages deal with human mortality in general rather than the mortality of the rich in particular.

1.11 James continues his reflections on the fate of the rich. Those who have nothing else to take pride in except their riches are compared to the wild flower which will encounter the *scorching heat* of the sun and so wither. Its beauty is lost *for ever*, with no trace remaining. The same fate awaits the rich man even *as he goes about his business*. This saying reflects something of the same thought as we find in the story Jesus told of the man whose life was demanded of him at the very moment he was congratulating himself on the success of his business enterprise (Luke 12.15–21). In the light of this teaching, it is difficult to credit that some Christians apparently teach that a person's wealth is a sign of blessing from God and that to possess it is a sign that one has been living faithfully and obediently.

Have they never heard the Epistle of James? Or have they heard it and failed to realize that hearing is not enough (1.22)?

1.12   So far James has introduced three basic topics, all of which will be expanded later in the epistle: the need to remain firm under trials, the need to ask God for the wisdom we need, and the question of wealth and poverty in the Christian community. With this verse he begins an expansion of vv. 2–4, on the nature of trials and temptations and their outcome. *Happy is the man* repeats the emphasis in v.2 on considering trials as a blessing or an opportunity rather than as a hindrance, but a further dimension is now suggested. It has already been said that such trials can refine faith, leading to fortitude and wholeness of Christian character. Here however, the emphasis is on the one who *stands up to trial*. This is a fairly commonplace thought in Jewish writings, especially those of an apocalyptic nature. A background has been suggested in Dan. 12.12, where there is a blessing pronounced on those who exhibit patient endurance in a long period of waiting until persecution ceases,[24] but the idea of blessedness being the lot of those who choose the way of the Lord rather than the way of sinners is more generally found elsewhere in the OT, especially in Psalms (e.g. Ps. 1.1; 34.8; 40.4), and in the Wisdom literature. The theme of being blessed when persecuted in the cause of right is familiar from Matt. 5.10. *Having passed that test* could be slightly misleading. Certainly there is the thought of trials which must be successfully endured, but the idea is really that of allowing the endurance which such trials produce to lead to the person who undergoes them being proved, and thus approved by God. NJB's slight paraphrase brings out the sense well enough: 'Such a person is of proven worth.' The word for 'proven' (Gk.*dokimos*) is frequently used by Paul, who can refer to someone being 'well proved in Christ's service' (Rom. 16.10), human approval for those who behave well (Rom. 14.18), and the way in which sectarian divisions in the congregation enable those who are genuine or proven to be recognized (I Cor. 11.19). As a Christian worker, Timothy is encouraged to show himself approved in the sight of God (II Tim. 2.15). For James, those whose who have endured their trials *will receive in reward the life which God has promised to those who love him*. REB oddly omits the word 'crown'. We should read: 'will receive in reward the crown of life which God has promised to those who love him.' Mayor suggests four crowns which James might have had in mind: (i) the victory wreath from the Greek games as in I Cor. 9.25 and

II Tim. 2.5; (ii) adornments which improve the wearer, as in Prov. 4.9 and Song of Sol. 3.11; (iii) a public honour for distinguished service, common in many Greek inscriptions and (iv) a symbol of royal or priestly dignity, as in II Sam. 12.30, Ps. 21.3 and Zech. 6.11. However, as Mayor also says, 'probably the metaphorical use would be coloured by all the literal uses'[25] and it is not strictly necessary to decide between them. The phrase 'crown of life' was a more or less stereotyped expression for the ultimate reward[26] and is used in the same way in Rev. 2.10 to encourage members of the church of Smyrna to be faithful to death, that is to martyrdom. It is in essence, whatever the background, a promise of a crown of glory in the future. This does not refer to any specifically recorded promise, still less to any 'lost' promise of Jesus, but is the natural outworking of the nature of the God who keeps faith with those who love him (Exod. 20.6). This passage in James, as in the other NT examples, looks forward: the death of those whose discipleship indicates their proven worth is followed by a crown of *life*. There is certainly a contrast here with the fate of those who rely on their riches, who merely 'fade away' (v.11). Christians have sometimes been accused of commending virtuous behaviour for the wrong reason, because it will lead to an ultimate reward, rather than because, as the essayist R.W. Emerson put it, 'The only reward of virtue is virtue.' But heavenly rewards (see Matt. 6.1–3) surely come, as C.S. Lewis observed, into the category of those 'rewards which do not sully motives.'

1.13   With this and the following verses, we come to one of the most perplexing passages in the epistle. The general sense seems straightforward enough, but when the text is examined in any detail it proves not to be so. A major problem is caused by the fact that the same Greek word can be translated both 'trial/test' and 'temptation', with a whole range of usages in which those meanings shade into each other. The difficulty can be illustrated (though not solved) by recalling the Lord's Prayer, where the same word is used (Matt. 6.13; Luke 11.4). The 'traditional' text of the Lord's Prayer runs: 'lead us not into temptation', which has often been felt to create difficulties, not least because of what James says here. However, the search for a widely acceptable translation into contemporary English has not met with much success. When the International Consultation on English Texts (ICET) proposed 'Do not bring us to the test', it evoked a mixed response. When preparing the *Alternative Service Book* (1980) the Church of England first adopted a different reading, 'Do not bring us to the time of trial', (which was printed in the *Methodist Service Book*, 1975, J1), then looked at possibilities of paraphrase such as 'keep us in trials of faith', and finally reverted to the wording of the 'traditional' text.[27] In verses 2 and 12, REB correctly translates the word 'trial(s)'. Why then, should a word from the same root require the translation 'tempted' in verses 13 and 14? Many commentators simply treat this as an example of one of James' 'catchwords', where the close relationship between the two words, rather than any common meaning, links them together. Dibelius characteristically comments: 'Therefore our saying can neither be combined with what precedes, nor be interpreted in accordance with it'[28] and argues for a sharp distinction between the 'trial' of v. 12 and the 'temptation' of vv. 13–14, and most commentators have broadly agreed. More recently however, P. H. Davids has argued for a quite different interpretation. Pointing out that if in this verse James is referring to the fact that God does not tempt people, he is merely repeating a common Jewish maxim and that this hardly fits his context, Davids suggests that James here continues to refer to *testing*. True, the Jewish tradition specifically says that God does test people (Gen. 22.1; Deut. 8.2 etc), but in later Judaism there is a tendency to find another source for such testing – Satan. Such a tradition makes it possible to blame an external force (God or another) for failure in the test, and James is naturally anxious to deny this possibility.[29] This suggestion is quite plausible and certainly has the merit of seeing this verse as a development of the preceding one. However, his further suggestion that the phrase *for God cannot be tempted by evil* means 'God ought not to be tested by evil persons', even though it draws upon an important theme in OT theology, summed up in the command: 'You must not put the LORD your God to the test as you did at Massah' (Deut. 6.16), is much less convincing. Unfortunately, it is much easier to criticize suggested explanations of this verse than to suggest a more convincing one! It does not seem possible to pinpoint precisely what James is saying here, but a rather free paraphrase may give the general sense: 'No one who is being put to the test, should say, 'It is God who is tempting me (so that I will fail it)'; God cannot himself be tempted by evil, so neither does he tempt anyone himself.' This raises the perfectly natural question: in that case, where *does* the temptation to turn aside in the trial, to give up rather than to endure, actually come from? James is not writing a treatise on how it is possible for evil to have entered into a world which God originally made good (Gen. 1.31), but he does have access to Jewish traditions which help him answer that question, at least sufficiently for his own immediate and practical purposes, and to these he turns.

1.14   The *temptation* (to do those things which would cause a person to fail in the test) comes when *anyone is lured and dragged away by his own desires*. These temptations, then, come not from without (not an external tempter, much less God), but from within the person. There is a quality within human beings (James is not especially concerned to discuss how it got there) which means that spiritually good things are not achieved without a struggle, and the outcome of such a struggle cannot be taken for granted. A person's *own desires* cannot be simply equated with sexual urges, as the AV rendering, 'drawn away of his own lust' and the imagery in the next verse of conceiving and giving birth, might superficially suggest. Underlying this text is the teaching of the Jewish rabbis concerning the 'evil inclination'. This was known as the *yēṣer* (from the Hebrew root 'to form') meaning that which is formed in the mind or, in other words, a person's imagination or intentions.[30] The word occurs in Gen. 6.5 where it is said that the Lord saw how human inclinations were always wicked, and therefore purposed the judgement which resulted in Noah's flood. It is found again in Gen. 8.21, which represents God as saying that however evil human inclinations may be, such a judgement will never befall the creation again. The *yēṣer* thus provokes both judgement and mercy from God. Later Jewish thinking developed both sides of this equation, and acknowledged human responsibility for giving in to the evil inclination:

> When in the beginning God created the human race,
>   he left them free to take their own decisions:
> if you choose, you can observe the commandments;
>   you can keep faith if you are so minded.
> He has set before you fire and water:
> reach out and make your choice. (Ecclus. 15. 14–16)

Like the notion of 'double-mindedness' (see the comments on v.8), this idea strongly implies the need to make choices. If the evil inclination is allowed to predominate, the result will be that temptations will be given in to, when they should be resisted.[31] It is just possible that Paul is working from a similar background of rabbinic theology in Rom. 7.19–23, with which this passage may be compared. Of course, James is not attempting to supply here a fully-fledged theology of sin and redemption any more than of the origins of evil itself. He does, however, remind us that however difficult it may be, any adequate understanding of discipleship has to reckon on the reality of the evil inclination in human beings, and on their propensity to be *lured and dragged away* from the path of true endurance by it. It can never be satisfactory for a person to say: 'Because this is what I am like, it is also how God wishes me to be.'

1.15   This inclination *conceives and gives birth to sin*, from which we note that the inclination is not necessarily sinful in itself, but if unchecked may become so. The slightly odd hunting and fishing metaphors of the previous verse here give way to an explicitly sexual one. Although 'desires' cannot be simply equated with sexual longings, they certainly include them. That though, is not quite James's point here: he means that giving in to the evil inclination is not the end of the matter. The desires which may be good in themselves then give birth to sin, which is as it were, bigger and stronger than its parent, and grows up to full maturity, to breed in its turn. The offspring of sin is *death*. Few biblical ideas sound stranger in the ears of twentieth-century people than this connection between sin and death. In an over-populated world we hardly question that one generation must make room for another, and we have come to regard death, at least when it takes place in old age, as both natural and inevitable. We cannot envisage a world in which everyone might live for ever, nor do we particularly want to. Yet the notion that death is profoundly *un*natural is deeply embedded in the biblical thought-world, and we need to understand why. The prohibition of Adam eating of the fruit of the tree of the knowledge of good and evil in the story of paradise, has the attached warning, 'the day you eat from that, you are surely doomed to die' (Gen. 1.17). This understanding is not a primitive one which the NT abandons. Indeed, it lies behind some of Paul's writing, including the idea that Jesus as the 'new Adam' reverses the effect of the first Adam's disobedience (Rom. 5.12–17; I Cor. 15.21) which is inexplicable without such a background. It also accounts for Paul's vivid description of death, not as a natural process, but as the 'last enemy to be deposed' (I Cor. 15.26). Although James does not make the same theological connections as Paul, he certainly assumes the same basic principle: *sin when it is full-grown breeds death*. If we find this strange, it is perhaps because we have paid insufficient attention to the biblical idea that 'true life was life lived in fellowship with God, and was hence indestructible.'[32] That, certainly, is part of the meaning of the story of Adam's disobedience, and of Eve's too. When they ate of the forbidden tree, they broke their intended relationship with God and one result is human mortality. We would hardly want to express the thought in exactly the same way today, but the truth itself is still important. The truly unnatural idea is that human beings, with all their longings and aspirations, exist only to be snuffed out in death. James has already reminded his readers that those who have proved themselves in time of trial will receive the gift of new life in the future (v.12). He thus declares, though in language rather different from that of Paul, that in the gospel, a generously-giving God also bestows the gift of a new future which continues from this life to the next.

1.16 This has been described as a 'hinge-verse' and it seems to operate in both directions. *Make no mistake*, appears to refer back to the statement that God does not tempt anyone in v. 13, and also forward to the contrasting idea which follows. It was a fairly common formula in ethical teaching of the time, sometimes used when a quotation was being introduced into the text, as in I Cor. 15.33 (see also I Cor. 6.9; Gal. 6.7).

1.17 If it is important to recognize that God is not the source of any-one's temptations, it is even more important to understand what does come from God; *every good and generous action, and every perfect gift*. This may well be a quotation, perhaps of a Hellenistic Jewish proverb familiar to the readers. It has often been noted that the phrase is in the form of a hexameter (a line with six measures, common in Greek poetry), even if a slightly imperfect one. This strengthens the case for regarding it as a quotation. However, the grammatical construction is somewhat awkward (literally: 'every good gift and every perfect gift is from above') which has given rise to the suggestion that James has slightly altered the original to fit his purposes. Be that as it may, REB offers a rather free rendering, for *action* does not appear in the original. Whatever the specific diffi-culties, the general meaning is clear: the good gifts which come the way of human beings have God as their originator. Such a God can be described as *the Father who created the lights of heaven*. Once again REB offers a free version, but with justification. The text reads, 'the Father of lights', and the phrase is not found anywhere else in the NT. Some versions render it literally (AV, RV, RSV, NRSV); others, especially more recent ones, often give it a reference. So we have: 'the Father of the lights of heaven' (NEB); 'the Creator of the heavenly lights' (GNB); 'the Father of the heavenly lights' (NIV) and 'the Father of all light' (JB/NJB) in addition to the REB. Of these JB/NJB is certainly misleading; the phrase cannot be taken in a somewhat Johannine sense to mean that God is the source of light as opposed to darkness, as this seems to do. It is significant that nearly all these translations insert 'heaven/heavenly', because the background to this phrase is broadly astronomical. James is thinking of the way in which the heavenly bodies, sun, moon and stars, are evidence of the Father's creative activity, designed for human good. We find this expressed in the wisdom literature (Ecclus. 43.1–10, e.g. v.2: 'The sun comes into view proclaiming as it rises how marvellous it is, the handiwork of the Most High'). In God's first speech to Job, the morning stars rejoice in God's creation before any human beings exist to do so (Job 38.7), and the existence of the heavenly bodies is an obvious reason for praising the love of God which endures for ever (Ps. 136.7–9). The description of God as *Father* here has, of course, nothing to do with the Christian doctrine of the Trinity as such. The thought is of God's creative activity, undertaken not out of mere whim or sport, but as an expression of parental love. The description of God as the Creator of the heavenly lights leads to a further assertion derived from the same metaphor: *With him there is no variation, no play of passing shadows.* The REB footnote indicates that some manuscripts have a different text, which can be translated 'With him there is no variation, or shadow caused by change.' In fact, the majority of manuscripts offer what is here relegated to a footnote, and that reading is to be preferred. Either way the phrase is so difficult that to make very precise sense of it a number of commentators suggest emendations to the text. However, to search too diligently for precise astronomical references (solstices, eclipses or anything else) may be to press the point too far. Although the sun, moon and stars are evidence of the Father's creative love for humankind, they appear changeable as we observe them from planet earth. The sun rises and sets, the moon waxes and wanes, the stars appear to shine more brightly on some nights than on others. The Creator, however, does not change. The Father who created the heavenly bodies, and all else besides, is entirely constant in attitude towards his creation, including human beings. The Epistle of James has probably not inspired very many Christian hymns, but the affirmations of this verse (and Lam. 3.22–23) are clearly the origin of the popular contemporary hymn, 'Great is thy faithfulness' (*Hymns and Psalms* 66).

1.18   The thought of God's creative activity is developed further in this verse. There was, so to speak, no compulsion on God to create human beings nor, when they had been created, to do anything further for them. All that was God's *own choice*. As Moltmann observes, 'when we say that God created the world "out of free-dom", we must immediately add "out of love".'[33] But is this what James is referring to when he adds, *he brought us to birth by the word of truth*? At first sight it looks to be so. The notion that the creation of the world is due to the will of God is common in the OT, especially in Psalms (Pss. 33.6–9; 148.5–6) and such a sense seems to follow on naturally from the previous verse. If this is what is meant, then the reference is 'to the original creation of which man was the crown and the promise'.[34] However, this scarcely does justice to the phrase *he brought us to birth*, which is an arresting image on its own account. The imagery is feminine (only females can give birth), and the fact that it is often overlooked is a gentle reminder of the way in which biblical texts have often been translated and read largely through masculine eyes (cf. AV, which translates: 'begat us'!). In fact, it is far from unparalleled in the OT (see Num.11.12; Isa. 66.13; Ps. 90.2 and, more remotely, Ps. 22.9). But it is another of the OT parallels which provides a second possible interpretation of the text here: 'You forsook the Creator who begot you and ceased to care for God who brought you to birth' (Deut. 32.18). Those words, bringing together both the masculine image of begetting and the feminine one of birthing, refer to the people of Israel as a chosen people of God. This would also fit with the purpose James ascribes to God's action, *to be a kind of firstfruits of his creation*, for Israel is so described in Jer. 2.3. It cannot be denied that this may have been in James' mind, and would have been readily enough understood by his Jewish Christian readers. However, it seems likely that the *birth* primarily intended here is the 'new birth' of Christian salvation. There are three reasons for thinking this. In the first place the Greek which is translated *brought us to birth* is not the more usual terminology (as in say, John 3. 3–8), but the word which James has already used in v.15, where it is said that full-grown sin produces death. The word is not found anywhere else in the NT, and James clearly intends a parallel between the two verses. This can only mean that God produces the opposite of death, new life or spiritual rebirth. In the second place, the text describes this being brought about *by the word of truth*. Such a phrase is found in II Cor. 6.7, Col. 1.5, Eph. 1.13 and II Tim. 2.15 where in each case it is synonymous with 'the gospel'. Since it means 'the gospel message' in its only other NT occurrences, it would be rather strange if it meant anything else here, and there is no very good reason for supposing that it does. Thirdly, the idea of being *firstfruits*, though applied on one occasion at least to the people of Israel, is also a term picked up in the NT tradition and given to the first Christian converts in their localities (REB translates it 'first converts' at Rom. 16.5 and I Cor. 16.15). In Rev. 14.4 it is applied to the 144,000 who follow the Lamb wherever he goes, and in II Thess. 2.13 (less certainly, for it is omitted by important mss) to Paul's converts – see REB marginal reading. We are justified then, in taking this verse to be a reference to the greatest of the perfect gifts which a loving Father bestows upon human beings, the gift of new birth which comes about when anyone hears and responds to the message of the gospel. We should not then miss the implications of describing Christians as the *firstfruits* of the new creation: such a perspective points to a harvest yet to come, the intention of a good and gracious God to redeem all humanity.

1.19   *Of that you may be certain* is an attention-grabbing phrase. But does it refer to what James has just written in vv. 16–18, or to what he is about to write in vv. 19–21? To put it another way, should we translate: 'Of *that* you may be certain', or 'of *this* you may be certain . . .'? There are varying readings in the Greek manuscripts and it is hard to be sure which is right. The majority of translations opt in one form or another for the second of these alternatives, with only RV, NEB and REB unequivocally choosing the first. On the whole, the second is to be preferred, A new subject is being introduced, not totally discontinuous with what has gone before, but coming at things from a new perspective. It is also not clear whether the opening word should be understood as an imperative ('Be sure of this!') or an indicative ('You may be sure of this'), though in view of the writer's fondness for opening new subjects with imperatives it is most probable that he intends one here. NIV's 'My dear brothers, take note of this . . .' catches the sense well, including as it does, James' characteristic mode of address (see the comments on 1.2). Why though, does he introduce such seemingly commonplace themes as listening, speaking and being angry in this context? Suggestions that it is an exhortation to be *quick to listen* to the gospel, the word of life of v.18, but *slow to speak* because not many of them ought to become teachers (3.1) are superficially attractive, but unlikely to be right. It is not hard to show that careful listening and speaking are characteristic concerns of the Jewish wisdom tradition, and this phrase may also be a quotation, or at least a reminiscence of a saying such as 'Be quick to listen, but over your answer take time' (Ecclus. 5.11; see also Prov. 10.19). The topic of the right use of speech was frequently discussed in Jewish circles, and James has much more to say about it later on. Interestingly, Prov. 17.27 makes a link between using few words and keeping a cool head, and the addition here of *slow to be angry* to the usual pairing of hearing/speaking may reflect a knowledge of the teaching of Jesus recorded in Matt. 5.22. In that passage, anger against another is associated with calling someone 'fool'. Although at one level what James says here is a commonplace of rabbinic and wisdom teaching alike, it is also clearly intended to be seen as an indication of how those who have been brought to birth by the word of truth should now behave. There follows a further indication of why anger is particularly to be avoided.

1.20   Given the interest in the topic of human anger within Jewish rabbinic and wisdom writings, we might expect there to be more in early Christian ethical teaching than is actually to be found. There are passages which deal with what we may regard as the working out of anger in specific contexts (such as the material on revenge in Rom. 12. 17–21), but remarkably little on anger in a less concrete sense. In Tit. 1.7 it is said that a church leader ought not to be 'short-tempered', but otherwise only Eph. 4.26,31 and Col. 3.8 provide any kind of parallel. In both those passages anger is a quality which Christians are urged to banish from their lives, with the specific suggestion in Ephesians that anger may turn into sin, and thus provide a foothold for the devil, if it is not dealt with by the end of the day. James however, sets the topic in the context of God's purposes for human life: it does not *promote God's justice*. The word which REB here translates *justice* is translated as 'righteousness' in 2.23, where it comes in a quotation from Genesis. It is usually assumed that James is referring to the righteousness which God requires from human beings and is to be understood as the exact opposite of 'committing a sin' in 2.9. In this case, the meaning would be that an angry person cannot perform the actions required by the law of God. That may be so, but there is something to be said for taking it in the sense adopted by REB. In 3.6–18 James writes first about the evils which can be attributed to an unbridled tongue, and then about the need for right conduct, illustrated by the replacement of jealousy and rivalry with peace, sincerity and kindness. True, anger is not mentioned again in those verses, but cursing others is (3.9–10). The desirable qualities which come from wisdom in 3.17–18 presuppose relationships in the community which are free from anger and all that it brings with it. It is certainly possible that here too, James' characteristic concern about the quality of life within the Christian community is in mind, and he is aware of what is produced by anger. In this case what is meant is something along these lines: human anger does not promote the standard of behaviour which should characterize membership of God's just community.

1.21 Instructions on the standard of behaviour expected of Christians is continued with the injunction to *discard everything sordid, and every wicked excess.* Most commentators rightly note that this is the sort of language widely employed in NT ethical teaching, especially when making the contrast between a person's conduct prior to becoming a Christian and that which is appropriate afterwards. It is not just a matter of whether a particular action or habit is or is not now acceptable, rather the thought is of an entire change of life. It is sometimes called 'putting off' language, because the picture is of taking off an old character as one might strip off old, dirty or unsuitable clothes. Good examples are found in Rom. 13. 12–14; Eph. 4. 22–24; Col. 3.8–12 and I Peter 1.25b-2.1. The last example is particularly close to what we find here, because the doing away with the old way of life is specifically related to receiving the 'word' and believing it. In several of the passages cited, 'putting off' is followed by 'putting on' the new nature which belongs to Christians, identified in the Romans passage with Christ himself. In some later Christian liturgical practice all this was dramatically symbolized by the practice of having candidates for baptism leave their old garments at the side of the baptismal pool in order to be clothed in new, white garments as they emerged.[35] Baptism however, is not in mind here, and the 'putting off' language is not followed by 'putting on' but by something different. The *sordid* things which are to be discarded are morally unclean things in general rather than any specific vices, but *and every wicked excess* is a little harder to interpret. The word (Gk. *perisseia*) means 'excess' or 'abundance', but the text can hardly mean either that wickedness consists in excess (as opposed to moderation), still less that wickedness is all right in small doses! Attempts to relate it to one particular vice, such as malice, are unconvincing. We agree with D. J. Moo that the word here stresses the variety and widespread nature of the sin which the readers must discard.[36] What we have here is not a demand for specific behaviour, but a summons to a whole new way of life. It is followed (reversing the order in I Peter 1.25–2.1), by the call to *meekly accept the message implanted in your hearts*. 'In your hearts' is not in the Greek text, but represents a particular interpretation of the meaning. More literally, the 'word' is said to be 'implanted' and this has caused some discussion. The Greek word so translated is found in a number of writers, but only once in the Jewish wisdom literature (Wisd. 12.10). It has been argued that it means, 'the original capacity involved in the Creation in God's image which makes it possible for man to apprehend a revelation at all'.[37] However, as Dibelius rightly saw, there are a number of problems with such an interpretation, not least that it is difficult to see how such a capacity could be said, in itself, to save souls. Moreover, the theme of 'hearing and doing' which is an important part of the context demands a reference to the 'saving word' which is the gospel.[38] This *message* is more than something innate or inborn which all human beings share. It comes from outside a person and needs to be accepted. James is not encouraging his readers to become Christians, they are that already. But when the gospel message has been planted in a human life it requires nurturing and tending in order that it may grow. Human beings may come to hold all sorts of views and beliefs without their making much ultimate difference to life. Not so with the gospel: it has *power to save* – already, as a new way of life is entered into, and ultimately, as the gift of God's new future. For that to happen, the acceptance has to be real, and James now turns to this point.

1.22   Genuine acceptance of the message is shown when those who hear it *act* in accordance with it. Merely to *listen* is to do no more than *deceive* yourself. There is a difference between being a 'sermon-taster' and a believer. Whether or not James is consciously referring to it, there is a strong association here with the way Jesus introduced the story of the two men who built their houses respectively on rock and on sand. He declared that those who would hear and act on his teaching were like the former, whereas those who would hear and not act resembled the latter (Matt. 7. 24–27) For James, the pattern

27

of Christian faith is emphatically not: first hear, then accept and finally practice. Rather, acceptance of the message is only real and complete when acting on it, living by it, and putting it into practice form part of the believer's lifestyle. James learned this from his Jewish heritage, and nothing in the good news brought by the Messiah Jesus caused him to change his mind. Paul certainly says something very similar when writing about how those within Judaism will be justified before God (Rom 2.13) and both writers reflect, though from different perspectives, something of the mind of Jesus (Luke 11.28).

1.23–25   Most books on the craft of preaching include a chapter on 'Illustrations', where writers on homiletics usually suggest that an illustration should only be used if it genuinely illuminates the point that is being made. At first sight it would seem that this is a lesson which James has not taken to heart! The general point is not difficult to grasp: it concerns the necessity for genuine acceptance of the message by acting on it, and it has already been well stated in v.22. Then we are presented with an illustration which, instead of making the point clearer, as a good illustration should, seems merely to confuse the issue. The person who *listens to the message but does not act on it* (which, as we have seen, thereby proves only that the message has not been properly accepted) is compared to someone who looks into a mirror at the face which is reflected there, but on going away forgets what the image looked like. By contrast, someone who looks into the *perfect law* and *does not turn away* remembers, acts on what is remembered, and so *finds happiness*. There is no doubt that this illustration of the mirror makes the passage more difficult. At the very least it seems to introduce additional contrasts of seeing and looking, of going away and not turning away, into the otherwise simple hearing/doing contrast. To add to the difficulties, whereas vv.23–24 seem to continue and in some way to illustrate the point of v.22, in v.25 a further person is introduced into the picture to contrast with the first. It is then clear that we have not one mirror, but two: the mirror in which the first person looks at *the face nature gave him*, and a second mirror which is *the perfect law, the law that makes us free*, for that too, can be looked into. A bewildering variety of explanations has been offered, including the counsel of despair that we cannot make sense of the text as it stands, but must accept that James was not very good at using illustrations! REB attempts to make some sense of the first contrast by suggesting that the person looking in the mirror merely *glances at himself* before going on his way, thus making it easier to understand that he *promptly forgets what he looked like*. Unfortunately, this does not help. The word which REB translates 'glances' can hardly mean that. Its common meaning is to 'look', usually 'look carefully', and it can accordingly mean 'consider/think' (see Matt. 7.3; Luke 12.24,27; 20.23; Acts 7.31,32; 11.6; 27.39; Rom 4.19; Heb. 3.1; 10.24). This man does not glance at his reflection, he looks carefully at it, yet still forgets what he looks like. How can this be so? It has often been pointed out that mirrors used in the first century AD were made of metal, not glass, that the cheaper kinds were especially liable to give a distorted likeness, and that they could become tarnished or rusty, but this does not seem to offer much help.

In an important piece of work, Professor Luke Johnson has investigated the ways in which the Hellenistic moralists regularly used the 'mirror' as a metaphor for moral instruction.[39] He shows that in much of the literature, mirrors were not simply treated as ornamental, or as luxuries, but as tools for self-improvement, precisely on account of their ability to reflect the human image. The moral teacher was often depicted as a kind of mirror in whom others could see themselves, and thereby recognize their need to improve. He offers a useful analogy from Epictetus, *Discourses* 11.14.17–23, where the philosopher has shown a man to be in need of the 'things most necessary and important for happiness', but concludes that the man has been done no harm thereby, 'unless the mirror also does harm to the ugly man by showing him what he looks like.' All the passages Johnson investigates show a combination of the mirror metaphor, the importance of 'remembering' and models to be imitated. The conclusion is that readers familiar with this idiom would (unlike ourselves) have no difficulty in understanding how James can use seeing and not acting/seeing and acting, and forgetting and not forgetting as related to one another. They are all basically related to the ability to see in the act of looking in a mirror, the need to recognize the need for self-improvement. In James' illustration therefore, the man who makes a careful observation of his features in a mirror, but then goes away and promptly forgets what he looks like, can be recognized as a man who has not properly used a mirror for self-improvement. Self-improvement in *this* case, would consist of turning hearing into doing. Once this is understood, the 'second mirror' becomes easier to understand. The *perfect law* supplies the person who looks into it, as in a mirror, the image of what that person now ought to become. The first mirror indicates what is lacking in the person who looks into it; the second mirror provides the models of moral behaviour to be imitated, thus indicating how what is lacking may be supplied. If this explanation is to be accepted, and it is by far the most convincing yet supplied, James has to be acquitted on the charge of being an incompetent illustrator and deemed, on the contrary, to be a very skilful one. The difficulties we experience in understanding it are due to the way in which illustrations which exploit contemporary literary devices lose their force when the background has been lost to us.

All this has important implications for understanding what James means when he speaks of looking steadily into the *perfect law, the law that makes us free*. Johnson suggests that the 'models of behaviour' which we would expect to find, given that the Hellenistic moralists always supply them when using this particular literary convention, are in fact Abraham and Rahab, Job and Elijah, who all appear later in the epistle. The case is perhaps easier to establish for Abraham, where the reader is asked, 'Surely you can *see* . . .' (2.22) and for Job, where the reader is told, '. . . you have *seen*' (4.11) than it is for Rahab and Elijah, but the idea is an interesting one. Although James may use a characteristic Hellenistic literary convention, he draws his examples solidly from the OT, and this may indeed have some bearing on what he means by *the perfect law*. Few things in the whole of the epistle are so disputed as what James understands by 'law', not least because he uses varying terms to describe it. Here it is both *the perfect law* and *the law that makes us free*. This latter description recurs in 2.12, but in the meantime there is a reference to the 'sovereign law' (2.8). In 4.11–12 there are references to 'the law' without any qualifying adjective. At least five different possibilities have been suggested for what James means by 'law',[40] but one thing is clear; James does not see the law as a problem. It sets free rather than enslaving, and it does so as it is obeyed. Yet such obedience to the law is not mentioned here as a matter of polemic, as if James were replying to someone who had asserted that the law *cannot* be thus obeyed. He regards it as quite natural that someone who has accepted the message planted in his or her heart, with all its power to save, should wish to look into the law and act upon it. Given the familiarity of James with the teaching of Jesus, especially the Sermon on the Mount, and his use of OT material, it is best to conclude that by 'law' James means the law which God gave through Moses (the Torah), redefined and reinterpreted through the Messiah Jesus as a 'new law'. To keep the law which God has given in this way will, naturally, enable us to *find happiness*.

1.26   The writer now provides another example of the necessity for true religion to be obedient religion. If some people think of themselves as *religious* – perhaps taking a pride in their own piety on the basis of the number of acts of worship in which they participate – well, there are tests of such piety. One test is whether such a person can *bridle his tongue*. If not, there is self-deception involved and such *religion is futile* or empty. If this particular example of empty religious profession seems a slightly odd choice, we must recall James' deep concern about the right use of speech and of the evils which follow from its wrong use (see the commentary on 1.19).

1.27   By way of contrast, *pure and faultless religion* (James is thinking of purity in its moral and ethical rather than cultic or ritual sense) has practical consequences. In v.26 'empty religion' refers to someone's self-estimate, but although human beings may deceive themselves in this way, and frequently do, they cannot so deceive God. What counts is whether something is real *in the sight of God the Father*. Here, as in 1.17, it is likely that James has particularly in mind God's work as the one who both creates and cares for his people, especially those who have no one else to care for them. This links well with the mention of *orphans and widows* who were an especially vulnerable group. Caring for them, along with strangers, was an important feature of OT religion (Exod. 22.22–24; Deut. 24.17–22). In the teaching of the prophets it stands as the mark of whether society is being run justly, in accordance with God's will (Isa. 1.17; Jer. 5.28). Indeed, God himself can be described as 'a father to the fatherless, the widow's defender' (Ps. 68.5). So here, care for this disadvantaged group is a mark of the reality of any religion worth the name and was certainly practised by the first believers (Acts 6.1–6). Although orphans and widows are not there singled out, the works of mercy for which the saved are commended in Jesus' picture of the judgement scene concern looking after those in various kinds of trouble (Matt. 25.31–46). To this description of a religion whose purity is shown by its practical and compassionate approach to the needy, James adds the requirement to *keep oneself untarnished by the world*. This seems to sit a little oddly alongside the previous clause which sees certain involvements in human affairs as praiseworthy.[41] It is probable though, that James uses *the world* to refer to that disposition in human nature and life which is antagonistic to God and to God's purposes.[42] It is certainly used that way in some parts of the Johannine writings (see I John 2.15–17). The 'worldliness' which James counsels his readers to avoid, consists in allowing yourself to absorb the values and standards of the society in which you live, in such a way that it is no longer possible to discern and live by the wisdom which God gives (1.5). In some Christian circles, 'worldliness' has frequently been defined in terms of specific behaviour, often related to quite trivial matters such as dancing or playing cards. But this is not the point at all. True worldliness is accepting those values and norms of society which have not been shaped by God's will. This verse almost irresistibly suggests a possible example: from the 'world's' point of view, there is no value at all in taking care of the poor and disadvantaged. They do not contribute to economic life and are a drain on resources. The world which operates apart from God's values will say, 'Let them fend for themselves.' Those who try to live by God's wisdom will say differently.

Love your neighbour as yourself
2.1–26

The first chapter of the epistle[1] appears to move with disconcerting suddenness from one topic to another. However, when we then read the remainder of the epistle we become aware that, to some extent at least, we are on familiar ground; there are no major topics which have not already been touched upon. The writer thus uses the opening chapter as a kind of expanded contents list. REB gives 2.1–26 the not inappropriate overall title 'Love your neighbour as yourself' which comes from Lev. 19.18 and is quoted by James in 2.8. The title encompasses two separate sections: 2.1–13, which develops the theme first announced in 1.9–11, and 2.14–26 which develops the theme first announced in 1.22–25.

2.1 The writer begins with a Christological statement, and follows it with an ethical demand; a connection exists between the two. First, the readers are addressed as those who *believe in our Lord Jesus Christ who reigns in glory*. The phrase runs so awkwardly in the Greek that it lends itself to several possible translations. A plausible case can be made for several of these, but none of them is self-evidently correct. AV and RV both translate, 'Our Lord Jesus Christ, *the Lord* of glory', making it plain that the phrase in italics is not in the Greek text and has to be supplied. RSV and GNB offer the same translation, but without the italics. All these take 'of glory' to refer just to 'Lord' in the Greek text. NIV and NRSV translate 'our glorious Lord Jesus Christ', which takes 'the glory' to refer to the whole phrase 'our Lord Jesus Christ'. Another possible translation would be 'our Lord Jesus Christ – the Glory', which has received the support of several distinguished commentators but is not adopted by any major biblical version. REB follows NEB and appears to adopt the 'Lord of glory' option, whilst at the same time offering an interpretation of what it means to speak of Jesus in such a way. What is in mind here is not the glory of God shown in the incarnate Lord (John 1.14), but Jesus as the exalted Lord. Crucified yet risen, he is now seated at the right hand of God, crowned with glory and honour, to use the language of the Epistle to the Hebrews. The rightness of this interpretation is confirmed by the stress later in the epistle on the Lord's role as the coming Judge (5.8–9). This idea of the Jesus who reigns in glory might seem rather remote from day-to-day concerns, but it is not. Such a description points to God's ultimate aim for a redeemed world (I Cor. 15.25), but it also reminds us that human life as we know it does not yet acknowledge the sovereignty of Christ. Part of the Christian task, therefore, is to live as those amongst whom the reign of Christ is a reality, so pointing forward to the ultimate hope for humankind. This is why James can move from an exalted Christological statement to a very practical demand. It is in the light of the fact that the readers *believe* in this exalted Lord that they are told *always be impartial*. Impartial seems rather a cold word and NEB's 'you must never show snobbery' more forceful. But the Greek word has overtones of looking only on the outward appearance when making a judgement. In view of the example which James gives next, REB was right to make the change. Human beings are all too prone to make judgements about the worth and value of others on the basis of whether they wear the right clothes, speak with the right accent, live at the right address or have the right colour of skin – 'right' of course being defined by the person doing the judging. That this is a foolish way to behave scarcely needs saying, but for James it is more than human foolishness, it is a denial of the reign of Christ. If Jesus the Messiah really is the crucified Lord then he was crucified for all. If he now reigns in glory then his reign is for all. For those who acknowledge his lordship the petty distinctions to which human beings cling so pathetically should have no force. They indicate nothing whatever about a person's value or worth, but merely hinder people from seeing what they have become in Christ – sisters and brothers. Paul says something not dissimilar in Col. 3.11. Having stated the principle, James offers an example.

2.2–4   *For instance* correctly indicates that what follows is not a literal description of something which has actually occurred, either in the home church or some other congregation known to the writer, but is a vividly drawn illustration of how the sin of 'partiality' might work in practice.[2] When we come to look at this example it is tempting to move too quickly to find parallels from our own experience or the recent history of the church, and then read them back into the text. We know of situations in which Christian congregations have been 'snobbish'. We may think of some church buildings which still display nineteenth-century boards proclaiming 'Free seats reserved for the poor' or, more proudly, 'All seats in this church are free.' We know that the wealthy have often been given special deference in the life of the church, no doubt because it was thought that they were in a position to further the church's interests. Some congregations, not least those in the deprived urban areas of Western societies, are accustomed to poverty-stricken strangers arriving for church services on a Sunday, often seeking some kind of practical help. If, as is often the case, they are unfamiliar with Christian worship, knowing neither where to go nor what to do, such a congregation may have to learn how to accept and welcome them in ways which are neither condescending nor judgmental. To read back directly from this kind of experience into what James is saying may however, be a mistake.

Who are these people who enter the *meeting*? REB prejudges the issues by describing them as *visitors*, but this is unlikely to be right. The text merely refers to two 'people' (literally: 'men'). When explaining what is wrong with the community's attitude, James says *you are discriminating among your members*, and it is very difficult to make sense of this phrase unless the two people who enter the meeting are themselves members of it (a similar problem of interpretation arises in connection with 1.9–10; see the commentary on those verses). We must also ask what kind of occasion is in mind here. James says that two people may enter your 'synagogue'. Some versions (RV; JB; NJB) retain this word, which is a reminder of the Jewish Christian ethos of the epistle. Others perfectly properly translate, 'gathering', 'meeting', or 'assembly', since it is not so much a building as a community which is in mind (in the same way, the English word 'church' refers to both the community of God's people and the building in which they meet). Whether this meeting is a purely Christian one, or whether it takes place in a synagogue attended by both Christian Jews and non-Christian Jews in the early years of Palestinian Christianity, it is impossible to determine. Is it a meeting primarily for worship, or for some other purpose? In an illuminating study, R.B. Ward has examined a number of texts in which the Jewish rabbis discussed the problem of partiality.[3] Nearly all of them refer to the need to avoid discrimination in judicial proceedings, and the parallels are striking. Such texts display considerable concern that justice should be equitable and that those involved should not suffer prejudice because of such matters as their outward appearance or the quality of their clothing. This is exactly what we find here, where the first person is never directly described as 'rich' but as *well-dressed with gold rings*, and the poverty of the second is indicated by his *grimy clothes* ('shabby clothes' would be better). The same rabbinical texts also instruct those in charge of such proceedings that favouritism must not be shown by assigning to a rich or powerful person a seat or a posture which would confer an impression of superiority, and thus an advantage. Again, this is precisely what we find here, where the first person is told *'please take this seat'*, but the second, *'you stand over there, or sit here on the floor'*. This background suggests that what James has in mind is not primarily a gathering for worship (though worship could possibly have been included), but a community meeting where issues of a judicial nature are being discussed.

If this is right, it is a reminder that the Christian community is to be seen as a body which can be trusted with disciplinary tasks, or even with making judgements about matters of dispute between its members. This is not unknown in rather different settings elsewhere in the NT. When Paul writes about the need to take disciplinary action against a church member involved in gross and unrepented sin, he clearly pictures the congregation assembled for just such a purpose (I Cor. 5.1–5). Evidence that the community might take on a semi-judicial role is found in the same Pauline letter, where the apostle chastises those who take their disputes to a 'pagan court' instead of allowing the Christian community to decide on the case (I Cor. 6.1ff.). It is Paul who provides the theological reasons for such a procedure (if they must go to law at all, let the judges be those whose understanding is shaped by the gospel), but the practice was evidently common. If we are to look for contemporary parallels with James, they would not be so much with a gathering for worship, as with a church meeting for business purposes. Actual disciplinary proceedings are fortunately rare, though most Christian bodies make provision for them as an ultimate safeguard, and in such cases what James has to say is directly applicable. Most congregations however, have meetings at which issues are discussed, views expressed and decisions taken. If such a gathering allows itself to attach undue importance to the views of those who have status and wealth, and correspondingly ignores those who are manifestly less influential, it may consider that it is *discriminating* among its members and *judging by wrong standards*.

2.5   The question which James poses in v.4 is a rhetorical one. Of course his readers know that to behave in such a way would be to judge by wrong standards, especially when the logical consequences of partiality have been stressed in such a strong and vivid illustration. Now he continues with another rhetorical question: *has not God chosen those who are poor in the eyes of the world to be rich in faith*? The writer is expecting no contradiction; his readers know this to be true as well as he does, but in reminding them of it he is providing an additional reason for avoiding the sin of partiality. Yet it is not immediately obvious to a modern reader why God should be said to have chosen the poor. The roots of this probably go right back to Israel's understanding of what God did through the Exodus. In Egypt *they* were the poor and oppressed, but God revealed himself as the saviour of an oppressed people because he saw their plight (Exod. 2.24–5). The deliverance from Egypt defined the character of their God and, correspondingly of their relationships with others. Some of the laws given in the Covenant Code reflect this awareness: 'You must not wrong or oppress an alien; you were yourselves aliens in Egypt' (Exod. 22.21, see also Lev. 19.9–10). As James Cone puts it: 'If God had chosen as his "holy nation" the Egyptian slave-masters instead of the Israelite slaves, then a completely different kind of God would have been revealed.'[4] This awareness shaped Israelite social behaviour. One mark of a good Israelite king was that he would use his power to look after the poor and needy (Ps. 72.12–14). The prophetic condemnation of the rich was not because riches are inherently bad, but because they were often gained at the expense of the poor (Amos 4.1–3; 5.11–12; Isa. 1.16–17; Jer. 5.26–28). In some strands of Jewish piety the term 'poor' came to be used as a synonym for those who were specially pious, because they depended on God alone. This seems to be the meaning behind such passages as Ecclus. 10.22–24, where material poverty is not primarily in view: 'The convert, the stranger, and the poor – their pride is in the fear of the Lord . . . The mighty, the judge, and the prince win great renown, but none is as great as he who fears the Lord.' At Qumran, members of the community retained their own possessions and looked after their poor, and at least one of their writings refers to 'the poor in spirit' in favourable terms.[5]

When we come to the NT it is not always easy to be sure whether references to poverty and the poor are meant to be taken in the literal sense or whether they have been spiritualized, even in Luke's Gospel, which has a special interest in the subject.[6] Here it seems that both senses are to be understood. To some extent material poverty must be involved because the poor person, discriminated against in the example James has already given, is clearly materially poor, and also because otherwise it is difficult to make sense of the intended contrast with the rich in the next verse. But 'poor in spirit', in the sense of 'pious' is also involved, since we are told explicitly that the poor have been chosen by God to be *rich in faith*. Perhaps James would have us understand God's choice of the poor in the light of the teaching of Jesus. It is likely that behind this verse is the beatitude about the blessings of poverty (Luke 6.20), which in Matthew's tradition has been modified to give it a more spiritual sense (Matt. 5.3). Just as Jesus promised the kingdom to the poor/poor in spirit, so here they are described as chosen *to possess* it. In many parts of the world, today's church has little option, because of the economic circumstances in which it is placed, but to be the church of the materially poor. Many of these communities are learning how the God of the Exodus, of Jesus and James, is still the God of the poor today, and are developing the resources of their members to become truly churches of the poor in spirit.[7] Those of us who belong to churches which are not in those terms poor (despite some economic worries), yet not always properly poor in spirit either, have much to learn from them.

2.6   We have already noted that the example in vv.2–4 is an imaginative illustration rather than a case-history. Nonetheless, as James proceeds it becomes increasingly difficult to resist the impression that some difficulties within the Christian community must have moved him to write in this way. Otherwise, it is difficult to account for the rather specific charge *and yet you have humiliated the poor man*. Granted that it refers back to the example, (and we could add after this phrase something like, 'if you have behaved in the way I have just described'), it is hard to see why such an elaborate example of discrimination has been offered unless it meant something in the experience of the readers. Perhaps the writer was aware of discriminatory behaviour creeping into some Christian communities. So he offers the strong words of vv. 1–5 to remind them that though it might seem only a trivial matter, it actually reaches to the heart of God's dealings with his people and of the whole nature of their relationships to one another in the community over which Christ reigns in glory. Further, discriminating in favour of the well-to-do is offensive for more than one reason. James must necessarily have particular situations in view when he writes about the rich being the *oppressors* of the Christian community. They are obviously rich and powerful people from outside the community, engaging in a measure of persecution. *Is it not they who drag you into court?* refers to something the readers know very well and have experienced for themselves. It is not possible to say whether such legal action was being taken specifically because the readers were Christians, or for some other reason. The Acts of the Apostles records such actions on purely religious grounds (Acts 4.1ff.), but also gives evidence that the Christian message clearly represented a threat to the commercial interests and profits of wealthy people (Acts. 16.16–23; 19.23ff.).[8] Perhaps the two are ultimately inseparable: it has often been the case that the very existence of faithful Christian communities has been seen as a threat by those whose way of life respects neither poverty nor piety.

2.7   Not only do the rich oppressors drag Christians into court, they also *pour contempt* (the word suggests verbal abuse, or blasphemy) *on the honoured name by which God has claimed you*. There is a rich OT background here, describing the close relationship between God and the chosen people. God has named his people as his very own (Deut. 28.10) and the idea recurs in the prophets when there is need for special reassurance (Isa. 43.1,7) or a time of special difficulty (Jer. 14.9). Indeed, there is frank recognition that at times in Israel's history it is only the fact that God has named them as his own which gives any ground for hope (Isa. 63.19). Here the implication is that the blasphemy and abuse is directed against the honoured name of Jesus, a precious name indeed for the believers, but quite the opposite for those who tried hard to prevent the apostles from preaching in 'that name' (Acts 4.18; 5.28). Willingness to name Jesus as Messiah would no doubt cause believers to be identified with that name in the minds of others long before the description 'Christians' spread from its origins in Antioch.[9] We would almost certainly be right to see a reference to Christian baptism in this verse.[10] Early Christian baptism (as distinct from various forms of baptism practised in Judaism, or later Christian baptism when the formula became Trinitarian) was administered in the name of Jesus (Acts 2.38; 8.16; 10.48; 19.5). Paul, giving an account of the aftermath of his Damascus Road experience relates how Ananias charged him to 'be baptized at once . . . calling on his name' (Acts 22.16) and it seems highly probable that in the earliest form of baptism the name of Jesus was 'called' over the candidate by the baptizer.[11] In the light of all this, it is quite astonishing that a Christian community should allow the well-to-do among them to have special consideration: such is the thrust of James' argument. Theological and practical reasons for shunning discrimination having been adduced, it might seem that the argument is concluded, but no: undergirding all these is the biblical teaching about love of neighbour, and it is to this that James now turns.

2.8–13 *'Love your neighbour as yourself'* is described as the *sovereign law*, and the readers are told that if they are observing it, *that is excellent*. The law has already been referred to as 'perfect' (1.25), that which 'makes us free' (1.25, see 2.12). Christians whose inheritance came from Judaism would naturally think in terms of the law which God gave through Moses (Torah), though certainly shorn of all its detailed ceremonial and cultic requirements (in which this epistle shows no interest whatever). Of course, they did not believe that keeping the law 'saved' them (neither is such a view to be found in Judaism at its best), but they naturally believed that in keeping it they were brought closer to the will and purpose of God for human life. In such circles there was no doubt an especial awareness of the way Jesus had dealt with the law. In that other Jewish-Christian writing, Matthew's Gospel, we find the sayings of Jesus about his relationship with the law most fully set out (Matt. 5.17–20).[12] We also find there a Jesus who taught and acted in ways which reinterpreted the law for his followers and restored God's original intention in giving it (Matt. 12. 1–14; 15. 1–10; Matt. 19.3–9, and the 'You have heard . . . but what I tell you' contrasts of Matt. 5. 21–44). Jesus also made it clear that *his* teaching carried authority (Matt. 7.21ff.). In those sayings which stress the continuing validity of the Torah, as reinterpreted by Jesus himself, we have the clue to what James has in mind here. The law is not the means of salvation (the 'implanted word' is that, 1.21) but to 'keep' the Torah as interpreted by Jesus was, within their tradition, part of the wisdom of God. It is significant that James here quotes the 'love command' of Lev. 19.18: *Love your neighbour as yourself*, and indeed it can be shown that this particular chapter of Leviticus has significance in several places in this epistle. The fact that the love command is quoted in connection with partiality in judging may reflect an awareness of Lev. 19.15, where the strictest *im*partiality is demanded.[13] This stress on the love command is very much what we find when we look once more at the teaching of Jesus. It is quoted by him on no less than five separate occasions (three in Matt. – 5.43; 19.19; 22.39, to one each in the other two synoptics: Mark 12.31; Luke 10.27); on at least four of those occasions we find it singled out as of special importance and on three it is linked with the command to love God, which is a consequence of confessing faith in the one true God (Deut. 6.4–5) . This is why for James it is the *sovereign* law; it has the impress of the Lord's authority upon it. It is at the heart of kingdom values.

It is tempting to conclude that James is arguing for the love command as the *essence* of the law, as if in keeping this command one would be keeping the entire law. However, in view of the way the discussion continues, this is probably not a correct conclusion.[14] James has in mind the whole law, as interpreted by Jesus. To keep it is to follow God's way of wisdom. It follows logically therefore, that *partiality* is a breach of this Christian sovereign law. As such, those engage in it are *convicted by the law as offenders*. There follows a 'hard saying', as thoroughly Jewish as anything in the epistle[15] and, at first sight a considerable problem. The difficulty consists not in what James means, for the sense of the words is plain enough: to fail in keeping the law, even in one respect, is the same as to fail in keeping all of it. The real difficulty for a twentieth-century Christian is to know how, if at all, such a statement has validity. Where, in this, is the Christian good news? The problem is lessened by remembering that it is not the entire OT law to which James refers, but to Torah as reinterpreted by Jesus, but it is not thereby entirely removed. It might be said that James has failed to detach himself sufficiently from his Jewish inheritance to realize that this kind of argument is no longer appropriate in a Christian setting. There may be a measure of truth in that, but it can hardly be the whole answer. It might also be said that if, on the contrary, the argument is judged appropriate for the Jewish Christian context of the epistle, it nevertheless ceases to be applicable in other circumstances. There may be a measure of truth in that argument too, but the logic of it must be that the teaching of Jesus, which forms and shapes this sovereign law, is no longer applicable either, which seems hardly tolerable. If there is a solution, it probably lies in the direction of remembering that this issue does not touch a Christian's *salvation*. Inasmuch as Christians are intended to live by the will of God (not as a condition of salvation but as a consequence of it), James' point still has some force. In Luther's famous phrase, we are 'at the same time justified, and yet sinners'. As such, no Christian succeeds in living fully by the will of God, and therefore all have continuing need of the grace and mercy of God. James' words, written against a rather different background to the one in which most of us live, may do us a service if they remind us of this truth.

James now cites the seventh and eighth of the Ten Commandments (or Decalogue), found in Exod. 20.1–17. The point of the citation lies in *for he who said . . . said also*: God is the giver of all the sovereign law, and if you break one of the commandments you have therefore broken the law itself, even if you have kept others of equal importance. Some commentators have discerned subtle reasons why these two particular commandments were chosen[16] but it is probably because they were recognized as weighty and serious ones. However, it is interesting that Lev. 19 (from which the love command is quoted in v.11), refers to six of the ten commandments alongside its often practical instructions. Two of the four *not* included in that chapter, are the seventh and eighth.[17] It seems as if James, expecting his readers to be very familiar with the Leviticus passage from which he quotes, then makes specific reference to some of the missing commandments. The association between the love command and the Decalogue was evidently a well-established one, appearing as it does in Jesus' reply to the rich young man, and in Paul's writings (Matt. 19.18; Rom. 13.9).

The final point in the biblical argument about love of one's neighbour now appears. The readers should ensure that their speaking and acting is undertaken as those *who are to be judged under a law which makes them free*. This 'sovereign law', the nature of which James has been expounding, sets people free in a way in which the law of Moses alone could not do. As reinterpreted by Jesus (e.g. 'the sabbath was made for man, not man for the sabbath'), it offers not a way of salvation, but an expression of God's will which should guide conduct. It is not to be seen as burdensome, for seeking to live by it should become the natural delight of those in whose hearts God's word has been planted (1.21). As D.J. Moo expresses it: 'God's gracious acceptance of us does not end our obligation to obey him; it sets it on a new footing.'[18] Nonetheless, it is important to remember that it is by our obedience or otherwise to the will of God that we shall be *judged*. No doubt there is a tension here, between on the one hand God's gracious acceptance of us though we cannot deserve it, and on the other God's judgement of us on the basis of what we do. If so, it is not a tension peculiar to James. It is present also in the teachings of Paul (contrast Rom. 5.6–11; 8.31–34 with Rom. 2.12–13;

I Cor. 3.13–15; II Cor. 5.10). Eph. 2.8–10 comes as close as anything in the NT, not to resolving the tension, but to giving proper expression to both poles of it and showing how they belong together. In this final judgement *there will be no mercy for the man who has shown none.* Judgement without mercy is a frightening prospect, but it remains possible for human beings to cut themselves off from the mercy which God desires to show, and one way of doing this is to refuse to show mercy to others. The intimate connection between showing mercy (to others) and in turn receiving mercy (from God) is found in Matt. 5.7, which surely lies behind what James says in v.13a. The principle is illustrated by the story of the unforgiving servant (Matt. 18.23ff.) and specifically referred to by Jesus in his teaching on judging (Matt. 7.2). Moreover, every time they pray the Lord's Prayer, Christians invite God to show them mercy in precisely the way they have shown mercy to others (see Matt. 6.12, 14). It is not a matter of an unmerciful God; it is a matter of whether a person's character has begun to reflect the very nature of God himself. As Barclay expresses it: 'If this mercy, this outgoing love, this self-identification with others is the characteristic of the nature of God, then he who has practised it in his life will become more and more like God; and he who has made no attempt to practise it in his life will become ever and ever more distant from God.'[19] James concludes on a note of hope: *Mercy triumphs over judgement.* This has the feel of an independent saying, quoted by James rather than written by him. The suggestion that it might be a saying of Jesus not recorded in the gospels[20] is an attractive one, and not inherently impossible. It certainly possesses the brevity and slight elusiveness characteristic of many of the best-authenticated sayings of Jesus. Its elusiveness is indicated by the difficulty of saying precisely what it means. It could mean either that in the final reckoning God's mercy will triumph over his judgement, or that human beings who are merciful to others will thereby avert an unfavourable judgement upon themselves. Given the context, the latter is perhaps slightly more likely.

2.14 James now begins to expand themes already announced in 1.22–25, mainly related to the need to act on the message which has been received. It is impossible to deny that there is some connection with the discussion on partiality in vv.1–13, but it is a rather indirect one. However, to give it a heading such as 'Faith and Deeds' in the manner of NIV or NJB, implies that it is a quite separate subject, which is misleading. James is concerned with how profession of faith is related to Christian behaviour, not as an abstract topic, but because of the need to know what loving your neighbour means within the community's life. The two previous references to faith have both been positive ones: faith may be tested and proved, and must be exercised in prayer (1.3,6). Now the reader is introduced to the idea that someone might profess faith without actually having it, or at least, without having what James regards as faith. *What good is it*, he asks, *for someone to say he has faith when his actions do nothing to show it*? The answer James expects is clearly, 'No good at all'. *Can that faith save him*? – again the answer is 'no' and the question is phrased in such a way as to expect such a reply. It seems that with v.14b we have begun to move into a different use of the word *faith*. It would bring out the meaning if we placed quotation marks around it ('Can that "faith" save him?') for James does not believe that such a faith is any real faith at all.[21] As such, and unlike true faith, it cannot *save* a person (linking back to v.13). James has now established that a saving faith is an operative faith which shows itself in deeds.[22]

2.15 An illustration now follows; as with that of vv.2–3 it is an example, not a concrete case. We may note that James is unconcerned here with the question of whether good deeds performed by someone who is not a Christian can lead to salvation. The picture is of a 'brother or sister' (REB's *fellow-Christian, whether man or woman* is an interpretation, but a correct one), who is *in rags* (literally, 'naked', but probably meaning lacking in the outer garment necessary to keep warm, especially at night-time). This brother or sister also has *not enough food for the day*. Although this is only an example, James' readers would no doubt recognize its essential truthfulness from their own experience; those in humble circumstances (1.9), and worse, comprised a high proportion of the early Christian congregations. None of the readers (or hearers) should have been in any doubt what the response *ought* to have been in such a situation, for clothing the naked and feeding the hungry is found in the biblical tradition as a definition of the kind of religious observance pleasing to God (Isa. 58.7). It also seems likely that we should read this illustration bearing in mind the works of mercy to which Jesus referred in the picture of the Last Judgement (Matt. 25. 35–6). There, it is precisely those who perform such works of mercy who receive favourable judgement, to their own considerable surprise.

2.16 The actual response to this situation of basic human need is depicted quite shockingly: one of you says . . . We might note in passing that James does *not* write (as he could have done), 'a wealthy member says'. *One of you* is, in effect, 'any one of you'. Believers are not excused from helping the very poor if they are in humble circumstances themselves, and we may recall that Jesus and his disciples, who certainly lived in humble circumstances, nevertheless had a common purse from which they gave to the poor (John 13.29). There is no giving to the poor here! Instead, someone says, *'Goodbye, keep warm, and have a good meal,' but does nothing to supply their bodily needs.* Whether this is to be taken as an expression of good wishes, or, even worse, as a kind of prayer (the words here translated *goodbye* literally mean 'Go in peace' and are probably best rendered as in NIV/NJB 'I wish you well'), the meaning is much the same. So is the effect: *what good is that?* It is certainly no good to the brother or sister who is destitute, and so to have said it is merely insulting. The good wishes are entirely hollow, a mere profession. Of course, James has already asked, 'What good is it . . . ?' when introducing his topic (v.14). His use of the identical phrase here rounds off the example in a neat way and provokes from the readers the same response – though by now surely even more strongly —'No good at all'.

2.17 Strictly speaking James has not so far been dealing with faith as such, but with someone who utters meaningless words – meaningless because they are not backed up by the only action which could give them substance. The application of this to the nature of faith itself can hardly be missed: *So with faith; if it does not lead to action, it is by itself a lifeless thing.* James is not offering anyone a choice between faith on the one hand and works on the other, he is demanding that the two be linked.[23] Any so-called faith which is not active in works of mercy is to be reckoned as no true faith at all. Any implied contrast in this verse is not between faith and works, but between a living faith and a dead faith.[24]

2.18 *But someone may say* introduces another voice into the discussion. Writers employing 'diatribe' form sometimes imagined another person who could bring forward a view contrary to that expressed by the writer. The argument then proceeded in dialogue with the imaginary other person. Paul does this in I Cor. 15.35 and elsewhere. Unfortunately, since the Greek manuscripts do not have quotation marks, James' use of this literary device creates some major problems. Who is this other person, and what exactly is being said? Where do the objections, and James' replies, begin and end? The arguments are very complex, and it is perhaps simplest to set them out in terms of four rather free paraphrases of the text, each along the lines of one of the possible solutions. Firstly, we might translate: 'Yes indeed! One might very well say, "You claim to have faith, and I have actions. Show me your faith without your actions, and by my actions I will show you my faith."' This way of looking at the text sees the 'other person' as being in agreement with what James has already said, reinforcing the argument which has been made. In this case it would refer back directly to v.14. It involves taking the opening word of the verse as intended to emphasize the argument, not to contradict it. This appears grammatically possible, if unusual. The major problem with it, is that in every other case where 'another person' is introduced in this manner, it is to express disagreement with what has gone before. If the author had wished to express what had just been said in different words the use of this particular literary device is an odd way to do so.

Secondly, we might translate: 'But someone will say, "*Do* you have faith, James?" I will reply, "I certainly have actions! You show me your faith without your actions, and by my actions I will show you my faith."' This way of looking at the text sees the 'other person' as a genuine objector, who is not raising a hypothetical objection to what James has said about the need for actions, but is rather questioning whether there is any evidence that the author actually possesses faith. There seem to be two problems with this. In the first place it makes part of James' reply redundant: all that needs to be said in reply is, 'I can show you my faith by my actions.' Furthermore, the notion of the 'other person' attacking the author in this way seems out of place in such a literary device.

Thirdly, we might translate: 'But someone will say, "You have faith; I have actions." In that case I will reply, "You show me your faith without your actions, and by my actions I will show you my faith."' This way of looking at the text involves no more than translating it fairly literally, and is adopted by NIV. It makes no sense at all. The difficulty with it is that we would expect the objection to be put exactly the other way round: 'You have actions; I have faith.' The objector is precisely *not* accusing James of having faith! Some have indeed suspected textual corruption at this point, but entirely without evidence.

Fourthly, we might translate, as does REB: *But someone may say:*

'*One chooses faith, another action.*' *To which I reply:* '*Show me this faith you speak of with no actions to prove it, while I by my actions will prove to you my faith.*' This way of looking at the text also sees the 'other person' as a genuine objector, but does not put any particular weight on the pronouns 'you' and I', taking them merely as equivalent to *one* and *another.* The problem with this view, is that the Greek pronouns do not normally mean this, and if this is the correct way to interpret the verse it has to be conceded that James is expressing himself very awkwardly. Moreover, the pronouns clearly revert to their usual meaning of 'you' and 'I' in James' reply in the second half of the verse.

None of these ways of reading the text is free from difficulties, but on balance it is probably best to follow REB and adopt the fourth solution. It has at least the merits of making the 'other person' a genuine objector and of making sense of the reply which follows. However, REB's introduction of 'chooses' is slightly unfortunate. 'One has faith, another action' would be better, because there may even be the suggestion that the objector is not so much actively hostile to James, as trying to put a balanced argument in response to what was said in v.17. As C.L. Mitton comments, 'Perhaps, it is suggested, some Christians have "faith" and others have "works"; and not all are expected to have both' – a view which could draw some support from I Cor.12.4–11.[26] It is important to note that the objector's statement posits a view of faith and action in which they are opposed to each other. This 'faith' excludes action and is supposed to exist without it. To this definition the author (the words *to which I reply* are not in the Greek, but have to be supplied), responds with a logical enough argument. If this 'faith' exists without any actions, how are we to know that it exists? It might be said, 'because I claim to possess it', but that is exactly the question at issue. Such a claim might well be meaningless, in the same way and for the same reason that the words in v.16 are meaningless, because nothing tangible exists to prove otherwise. In this sense the invisibility of any such claim to 'faith' speaks against its reality.[27] James is not saying that faith and works are dependent on one another and that the believer needs both; he is saying that a hypothetical faith, apart from the evidence of actions, is meaningless.[28] On the other hand, those who can point to their deeds of kindness, their loving actions, can justifiably claim that here is some kind of proof that their faith is real. REB places the speech marks at the end of this verse to indicate that James' direct reply to the objector is now at an end. This is probably right, though there is some sense that an another party is being addressed as far as the end of v.23. However, that makes no practical difference to how we understand the meaning.

2.19   The consideration of the nature of genuine faith is now continued, strengthened by the author's refutation of the possibility that it might exist without some form of action to prove its reality. *You have faith and believe that there is one God*, he says. This belief would undoubtedly be shared by both James and any objector, whether the reference is to a simple confession of faith that there is only one God (monotheism) or, more specifically, to the confession of faith of Deut. 6.4: 'Hear, Israel: the Lord is our God, the Lord our one God', recited twice daily by devout Jews. Such an understanding of the nature of God is foundational to any proper faith. It was endorsed as a matter of course by Jesus when he was asked which was the first of all the commandments (Mark 12.29) and appears several times in the NT as a basic truth for Christians (Gal. 3.20; I Cor. 8.4; Eph. 4.6). It therefore earns the commendation *Excellent!* Some commentators have discerned varying degrees of irony here, on the grounds that in the next words *even demons have faith like that* James appears to be discounting such a faith. This may be doubted; it is unlikely that the author would have been ironic or dismissive about so basic a belief. What he is really suggesting is that not even something as important as this is enough on its own. To confess that there is one God is indeed excellent, but it is only a foundation for something else, or perhaps a starting-point. If it remains a belief only at the level of intellectual conviction then it does not become wrong in itself, but the response is inadequate. This fits everything else James has said so far about faith. That the demons believe there is only one God is no more than a statement of fact, but in their case such a faith *does* produce action, of a kind appropriate to demons: *it makes them tremble*. Sophie Laws makes the important point that this picture of the way in which the demons respond to the reality of God may be compared to the way in which the demons recognize Jesus (Mark 1.24; 5.7), knowing that he has come to destroy them. She finds the background to James' illustration in the practice of exorcism, and this may well be right.[29] If then, the trembling of the demons demonstrates that *they* recognize the reality of God, would we not expect to see a demonstration of a different kind in the life of a human being who claims to believe the same thing? Well, of course, the answer is obvious: human beings who confess the reality of the one God are immediately told, 'and you must love the Lord your God with all your heart and with all your soul and with all your strength' (Deut. 6.5). When referring to that passage, Jesus added love of neighbour (see the commentary on vv.8–12). As we have seen already, James is interested in the nature of faith largely in terms of what it means to love your neighbour within the Christian community. His argument then, is all of a piece.

2.20 *Do you have to be told, you fool* . . . conveys the sharpness in the writing, and leads into the next section. Having demonstrated as logically as he can *that faith divorced from action is futile,* James sets out to back that up by appeal to examples from the OT. REB's *divorced from* is not the most natural rendition of the Greek which contains a play on two words and can be translated as D. J. Moo suggests, 'Faith which has no works does not work'! Literally, it is 'barren'.

2.21–24 The first example of what it means to have a genuine faith is that of Abraham. The choice is hardly surprising. In the Jewish tradition, Abraham was one of the greatest exemplars of the qualities of faith and obedience, especially obedience which is tested. The First Book of Maccabees records how the priest Mattathias, in a speech delivered shortly before his death, strengthened the determination of his friends and family at the beginning of the Maccabean war by reminding them of the heroes of the past: 'Did not Abraham prove faithful under trial, and so win credit as a righteous man?' (I Macc.2.52). The Wisdom literature similarly celebrates Abraham's faithfulness under test (Ecclus. 44.19–21) and Wisdom herself is said to have 'recognized one good man and kept him blameless in God's sight, giving him strength to resist his pity for his child' (Wisd. 10.5). These references are all primarily to the story of the testing of Abraham's faith which came through the command to sacrifice his son Isaac (Gen. 22. 1–18). However, in the Jewish tradition of interpretation, that story did not stand in isolation. It was seen as the capstone of a whole series of testings, ten in all, which Abraham went through, and in which he was shown to be faithful. This tradition is in James' mind when he writes that it was *in offering his son Isaac upon the altar, that our father Abraham was justified.* It has however been claimed that a rather different background must be sought. There was also a Jewish interpretative tradition which drew on the story of Abraham's hospitality in Gen. 18.1ff., and which saw him as the paradigm of the hospitable man. In this understanding the *actions* of Abraham to which James refers are 'works of mercy' which include the giving of hospitality to strangers.[30] This is an obviously attractive interpretation because it fits James' context of concern for love of neighbour, but there is nothing in the text to suggest that it is right. It could be, but we cannot be sure. In any event, it does not greatly help to solve what is perceived as the central problem of this passage. In saying that through his actions Abraham was *justified*, James appears to be in flat contradiction to Paul, who in Rom. 4.1–3 explicitly says that Abraham was not justified by anything he did, but by his faith, and quotes Gen. 15.6 in support of that view. Although suggestions that either writer is deliberately correcting the other are most unlikely (see the Introduction: 'James and Paul'), we cannot discount the possibility that they are in practice contradictory. Passages from different NT writers ought not to be harmonized on the basis of some theory that they cannot be allowed to contradict one another. Full weight must be given to the diversity of the New Testament witness. Equally, of course, it is unhelpful to assume that just because Paul and James use the Abraham material in different ways they necessarily contradict one another. Only examination of the text can decide the issue.

One suggestion which has often been made, is that Paul and James use the word *justified* in different ways, and to mean different things. As it is most often used, it refers to an act whereby God 'declares' a person to be righteous, that is, deemed to be innocent in his sight, and thus able to receive salvation. For Paul, God 'declared' Abraham to be righteous on the basis of his faith, the same basis as is now made available to all who put their faith in Christ (Rom 4.5). If James is using *justified* in this 'declaratory' sense (in vv. 24–5 as well as here), then it seems he must be saying that a person's actions are the grounds on which God declares him or her to be righteous, which would be clearly at odds with Paul's view. However, it has been argued that *justified* has another sense, in which it is not 'declaratory' but 'demonstrative'. In this understanding, the 'actions' demonstrate that saving faith already exists. If James is using the word in this 'demonstrative' sense, then the passage deals with showing the reality of an already existing faith (and therefore of salvation).[31] We could then paraphrase James' words along these lines: 'Was it not his action, in offering his son Isaac upon the altar, which demonstrated that our father Abraham was counted as righteous?' If this understanding is correct, it appears that James is not writing about 'justification' in the Pauline sense at all. But is it correct? It is true that *justified* appears to be used in this 'demonstrative' sense in Matt. 11.19; Luke 7.35; Rom.3.4 and I Tim. 3.16 (though the REB translates the first two of these with 'proved right'). However, the demonstrative sense is not the usual meaning and if James were using it in this less usual sense we might expect some indication that this is the case. Other scholars, accepting that James is here using the word in the 'declaratory' sense, have nevertheless tried to minimize the conflict with Paul by arguing that whereas when Paul uses it he is referring to the initial righteousness which God declares a person to possess through faith, James uses it to refer to the status of righteousness which God will confer in the final judgement. This view makes a distinction between 'initial justification' (Paul) and 'final justification' (James).[32] However, there is no basis for this interpretation in the text; both Abraham's action (v.21) and later on that of Rahab (v.25) appear to receive God's approval immediately, as well as, presumably, at the final judgement. If we are to understand what James means in this passage, it does not appear that we shall derive a great deal of help from examining the meaning he attaches to *justified*, because it is used here for the first time and we have nothing with which to compare it. A more fruitful approach is to return to his use of *actions* (deeds/works) and ask ourselves again what he understands by that term. In this connection it is noteworthy that the incident which James selects from Abraham's life (the offering of Isaac) is never adduced by Paul. However, as we have seen, the story of the offering of Isaac is used in the Jewish literature as the supreme example of how Abraham's faith withstood trials. More importantly for our present purposes, it is also cited in Heb. 11.17–19, and is used there as an example of Abraham's *faith*. That chapter opens with the statement, 'It was for their faith that the people of old won God's approval' (Heb. 11.2) and the writer goes on to draw a number of examples from the OT (including Rahab, whom Paul never refers to). Of Abraham he writes: 'By faith Abraham, when put to the test, offered up Isaac.' Strictly speaking of course, Abraham did not actually offer up Isaac, because at the crucial moment his hand was stayed (Gen. 22.12). The reference is to the 'binding' of Isaac preparatory to his being sacrificed, taken as conclusive evidence of Abraham's intention. Certainly for the writer to the Hebrews, Abraham's action in binding Isaac is seen as a manifestation of his faith.[33] This is very much what James says next: *Surely you can see faith was at work in his actions, and by these actions his faith was perfected*? A fairly literal translation of the first part of this would be: 'You see that faith worked with his works', or even, 'faith co-worked the works'.[34] For James, the story of the binding of Isaac is supremely an example of faith in action. It is perfectly clear how the Genesis story could be understood in this way, since it is presented as a 'test' of Abraham's faith (Gen. 22.1), and in the light of Abraham's obedience the angel of God says to him, 'Now I know that you are a godfearing man.' Abraham's action, in other words, demonstrates that his faith is not a matter of mere profession, but has substance and reality. The *actions* that James ascribes to Abraham are not therefore, keeping the law (Torah), nor even 'works of mercy', but the radical obedience of faith itself. Such an understanding fits well with what James elsewhere says about faith which is tested (1.2–3). It also fits with the fact that it is the 'objector' who defines faith and works as separate, distinct and opposed to one another (v.18), not James. He has consistently argued for the importance of actions, not as possessing saving value in themselves, but because their presence or absence demonstrates the reality or otherwise of faith. So it is here, and the quotation from Gen. 15.6, *Abraham put his faith in God, and that faith was counted to him as righteousness*, emphasizes the point. Abraham did indeed put his faith in God – but James' point is that the faith concerned was no verbal profession alone, but a real and living faith, tested and found true. Now when Paul quotes this same text he does not even consider the question of whether Abraham's faith was real or not, he takes it for granted that it was. James however, is writing in a quite different context, in which some people seemingly hold that faith unaccompanied by actions is still real and saving faith. He needs to show that this is not so. Only because Abraham's faith was living and fruitful could it be *perfected* in his actions (or, 'reach its goal in his actions'). It is in view of this, that James can say Abraham *was called 'God's friend'*, a familiar title for Abraham in Judaism, and possibly also connected with the view that Abraham was an apt exemplar of the truly wise man.[35]

From the example of Abraham, James draws the more general conclusion: *it is by action and not by faith alone that a man is justified*. The interpretation which sees this as a direct refutation of Paul (whether Rom. 3.20, 28 or 4.16, which are the most frequently cited texts in this connection) is made far less likely when we consider the context of James' concerns. He has indeed heard some such slogan as 'by faith alone', but it does not mean at all what Paul means by it, and it is probably not even from people who have heard Paul and misunderstood him. In the context of James'community the phrase means, 'we have made our profession of faith and in the sight of God that is sufficient.' But as has been argued (at least as far back as 2.1), those who think that it is possible to love God without loving their neighbours are wrong. God, James says, declares that people are righteous in his sight on the basis of genuine faith, not spurious faith. Though he speaks so much about actions, he does so only in order to define what faith means. Of course, many of the questions which spring to our minds are simply not dealt with here. James says nothing whatever about that important question in Paul's mind, whether or not the Gentiles need either the ritual law (such as circumcision) or the keeping of Torah in order to be saved. Nor does he say anything about whether God could declare to be righteous the person who has works but does not profess faith. Still less does he discuss such fascinating theological niceties as whether someone might be saved following a deathbed conversion, who therefore has no opportunity to demonstrate whether or not the profession of faith is real! We must not force on the text questions it was not designed to answer. To some extent, whether James is thought to contradict Paul must be a matter of individual judgement. But on the central issue, they are not writing about the same thing at all. James's great contribution to the Christian life is not on the doctrine of justification, but in helping us to see that true faith is radical obedience.

2.25   The second example is of *the prostitute Rahab*. Her exploits are recounted in Joshua 2. On the face of it, they seem to amount to little more than common prudence – common treason if looked at from the point of view of the inhabitants of Jericho! But in the Jewish tradition she came to be lauded as an example of a non-Jew who had come to put her faith in the God of Abraham, of Isaac and of Jacob: 'the Lord your God is God in heaven above and on earth below' she said (Josh. 2.11). The Epistle to the Hebrews includes her in the roll-call of the faithful, along with Abraham and, as in his case, sees her *faith* as manifested in her actions – in this case 'because she had given the spies a kindly welcome' (Heb. 11.31). Indeed, that same verse specifically differentiates her from the 'unbelievers' who perished in the destruction of Jericho. For James then, the example of Rahab makes precisely the same point as does the example of Abraham: taken together they show that the father of the faithful and the most illustrious convert both exemplify a living, active faith.[36]

2.26 We may wonder why James finds it necessary to say, once again, that *faith divorced from action is dead*, since nobody who has followed the argument thus far need be left in much doubt that this is so! The likely answer is that this is a reference back to v.17, and there is a reason for it. That verse refers to the importance of loving your neighbour in active deeds of mercy, as opposed to the shocking example of empty words which precedes it in vv. 14–16. By rounding off his two biblical examples in the same manner, James indicates that the context of the discussion has not changed. His interest in a faith which justifies is not theoretical, but is concerned with neighbourly love.

Christian speaking
3.1–12

The topic of Christian speaking was briefly alluded to at 1.19 and then more fully announced in the 'contents list' for the epistle at 1.26. It is worth noting that, of the three non-biblical illustrations James has used, two depict people speaking in ways which reveal that their 'faith' is not shown in love of neighbour (2.3,16). Speaking and acting are, for James, intimately related. Both are to be controlled by the law of love, and human beings will be accountable for both in the judgement (2.12).

3.1 The passage begins with a warning, for which a reason is then given. After addressing the community in his usual way, James warns: *not many of you should become teachers*. Teachers of Torah were held in considerable honour in Judaism. Students attached themselves to a particular teacher and accompanied him in the course of his teaching journeys, hoping to grow in wisdom and skill as they did so. The title of 'teacher' is given to Jesus more than thirty times in the gospels, often as a mark of respect, but sometimes with ironic intent by his opponents. Jesus, though, was no more a typical Jewish teacher than the disciples were typical students; their roles went far beyond that. However, the Johannine record does tell us of the occasion when Jesus accepted the disciples' application of the title to himself, whilst reminding them that his teaching was by example as well as precept and they ought to follow it (John 13.13–14). It is clear that the young Christian church quickly saw the need for authorized teachers of the faith, though it is rather less clear precisely what role they performed. There are many references to 'teaching' in the NT writings outside the gospels, but apart from James here, only four others to *teachers*,[1] and they merit some consideration. (i) In Acts 13.1, a group of five people, including Paul and Barnabas, are described as 'prophets and teachers'. It is not immediately obvious from the context whether all five were both prophets and teachers, or whether some were prophets and some teachers. This rather suggests that the distinction cannot be drawn too sharply, though we are told that Barnabas and Paul, chosen from this group for a missionary journey to Cyprus, had been exercising a teaching ministry within the church at Antioch, and would do so again when the missionary journey was completed (Acts. 11.26; 15.35). (ii) In I Cor. 12.28, Paul lists the gifts which have been bestowed by God upon the Corinthian church. Teachers come third, after apostles and prophets, and there is then a break before the remainder are enumerated. This almost certainly means that Paul regarded the first three as more important than the rest because they performed functions considered essential to the church's life.[2] However, the passage tells us nothing about the functions performed by teachers. (iii) In Eph. 4.11, teachers are again mentioned along with apostles and prophets, this time with the addition of evangelists. However, on this occasion the wording is different: 'some to be . . . pastors and teachers'. Here the two are linked together in one order of ministry.[3] This suggests that teaching forms a proper part of pastoral care, and also that teaching is in itself a form of such care. (iv) In Heb. 5.12, the author chides his readers for having been slow to learn anything other than the ABC of faith, telling them that they ought to be teachers themselves rather than still needing someone to teach them. This suggests that a primary function of teachers was to explain how the initial profession of Christian faith was to be worked out and understood in daily life. The statement that the readers ought themselves to be teachers is probably a description of the level of understanding all should have reached, rather than an indication that they should teach one another, though that possibility cannot be entirely excluded (Col. 3.16). It has been suggested that one distinction between apostles and teachers was that the former were itinerant, being chiefly concerned with proclaiming the Christian faith, especially to those who had not heard it, whilst the latter were attached to local congregations and charged with the task of building people up in their new-found faith. This is a perfectly plausible suggestion, though we lack the evidence to be certain that it is right. Luke describes how the apostles taught the company of believers in the earliest days of the church (Acts 2.42) and, as we have seen, Paul the 'apostle to the Gentiles' exercised a teaching function at Antioch; also, it appears, in other places (Acts 18.11; 20.20). Despite the distinction in terminology, it is best to regard the boundaries between the roles of apostles and teachers as being somewhat blurred, or perhaps appearing differently in different Christian communities.[4] The stress on the importance of faithfully transmitting sound and approved teaching was strong by the time the Pastoral Epistles were written (II Tim. 2.2).

In the Epistle of James that situation has not yet been reached, though it is evident that teachers were officially recognized, and their words carried authority, otherwise James would not write as he does here. Of course, teachers were necessary in any Christian community, if only to carry out the command of the risen Jesus not only to make disciples and to baptize them, but also to teach them (Matt. 28.20). That such a task involves heavy responsibilities is plain enough, and James counsels restraint in its undertaking. This might be directed against those who wish to become teachers for the wrong reasons. In a community where being a teacher confers status, unworthy motives for desiring it are always a possibility. In those Christian traditions where there is a high regard for the ordained ministry, much the same might still be said. Or is it possible that James is concerned lest too many people become teachers, resulting in confusion amongst the believers because of the multiplicity of conflicting opinions advocated by those to whom they look for guidance? That situation is hardly unknown in churches, now as then, and there is no solution to it unless those involved are prepared to trust each other's Christian integrity as part of the exercise of Christian love. Whatever the grounds for James' counsel, he is *certain that we who teach will ourselves face severer judgement.* We note that he includes himself in the company of teachers – the one piece of personal information the author gives us. The spiritual principle behind this may well be that from those to whom much has been entrusted, much will be required (Luke 12.48), though that saying is not directly in view here. Rather more in mind is Jesus' insistence that we shall be either acquitted or condemned in the final judgement out of our own mouths (Matt. 12.37).

Those who undertake a teaching role in the church are thereby entrusted with responsibility for the spiritual growth of others. To misuse that responsibility (whether by neglect, false teaching or the substitution of one's own opinions for the gospel) is a grave matter indeed, especially for those who know they must not cause others to stumble (Matt. 18.6). The complexities of the twentieth-century world have not made such work any easier. To teach the way of Christian wisdom in a multi-cultural society, where Christians cannot claim a monopoly on understanding, and to do so both sensitively and faithfully, is a difficult task. It is not made easier by those Christians who demand simple answers to questions which are anything but simple, or who expect their teachers to confine themselves to repeating the formulas in which faith was best expressed in the past. In including himself among the teachers, James gives some pointers as to how it might be done, and 'may provide in his own epistle the best example of the exercise of the Christian teacher's task'.[5] The author weaves together into one treatise the OT, the Jewish wisdom tradition, the teaching of Jesus, the 'perfect law', the received doctrine of God and the implications of believing in the Christ who reigns in glory. All these are related to the task of living faithfully in difficult circumstances, to personal relationships, the use of one's resources and the life of prayer. Such is the task of the Christian teacher.

3.2   The thought of judgement, and the awesome responsibilities which are laid upon Christian teachers, lead to a recognition that, however hard we try, *all of us go wrong again and again*. This is true not just for teachers, but for everyone. It is neither a counsel of despair, nor just a humble confession on the part of the author, but simple realism. Mere recognition of the responsibilities we bear does not of itself confer the power to exercise them well. For that, vigilance is required. James now appears to change tack somewhat, or at least, to broaden the range of his audience. Up until now he has had the problems and responsibilities of Christian teachers particularly in view, but from this point onwards the writing is much more general. Of course, what is said about the dangers of the unbridled tongue is applicable to Christian teachers because teachers work with their tongues, but it is also applicable to any Christian believer, whether or not she or he carries recognized responsibilities within the fellowship.[6]

The second part of this verse announces the subject which the succeeding illustrations will amplify: *a man who never says anything wrong is perfect and is capable of controlling every part of his body*. The commonplaces of *our* contemporary moral slogans include such elegant sayings as, 'Engage brain before opening mouth', and the comparison is not as flippant as it may at first appear. Words are often spoken without prior thought, and they may be spoken quickly, with no possibility of retraction. That other commonplace, 'As soon as I had said it I could have bitten my tongue out', makes the point, except that even such drastic action could only indicate the remorse of the speaker, not cause what had been said to be unsaid. James' point is not that sins of the tongue are *per se* more serious than any other sort of sin (which would be ridiculous), but that it is remarkably difficult never to say anything wrong, simply because of the ease with which speech occurs. Hence the assertion that if we were able to have our tongues under such control that we never spoke without first weighing the consequences, we would almost certainly be able to control those parts of our body which are less unruly than the tongue. If James' assertion at first seems like an over-statement, reflection on daily experience may help us to appreciate its truth.

3.3   What follows is one of the most recognizably Hellenistic passages in the entire epistle, with many of its illustrations and com-parisons being fairly frequent in the rhetorical writers. As such, they were probably also common currency as proverbs or sayings. James has not overtly 'Christianized' his sources; he can draw on the insights of the contemporary moralists where they are in conformity with the gospel he teaches, just as a Christian writer or preacher today might utilize a *Times* leader, or quote a recognized proverb, without demanding to know whether it is is explicitly Christian in origin. Speaking only in the 'language of Zion' is hardly good Christian communication. So here James uses language and imagery familiar to his readers in the situations in which they live. It has to be said that he is not always totally at ease with it and occasionally, as we shall see, seems slightly out of his depth. Preachers and teachers who have ever attempted to reach their audiences by using illustra-tions from a *milieu* in which they are not themselves entirely at home, will recognize the dangers! The illustrations used here are intended in each case to make the point that little things can have large consequences. The *bit* which is placed in the *horse's mouth* before it is ridden (or used to pull a chariot, which may be the thought in this instance), is very tiny. Nevertheless, by it *we can direct the whole animal*. The word for *bit* comes from the same Greek word as that which REB translates *controlling* in v.2, so it is possible that the word itself suggested the illustration to the writer.

3.4   Just as the bit controls the horse, so *a very small rudder* can steer a *ship* even though it is *large*. The reference to the ship being *driven by gales* means either (i) a large ship is driven by gales (which are large things) and also by their rudders (which are little things), or (ii) a large ship can be steered by its (little) rudder even in the teeth of the (large) gales which drive it; the Greek can be read either way. The second of these meanings seems marginally more likely, but the point is much the same in either case.

3.5   Up to this point, the comparisons have shown that even tiny things can have considerable consequences. However, James now says: *So with the tongue; it is small, but its pretensions are great,* and his slight unease with his material begins to show. In vv.3–4, it is the horse and the ship which are large and unruly, thus requiring control which they duly receive from the small bit and the little rudder respectively. From this we expect the writer to continue with something like: 'So it is with our bodies, we can control them with our tongues', but he does not. On the contrary, it is the *small* tongue itself which requires control. The illustrations do not fit exactly, though in general terms it is clear enough what is meant. The Greek phrase 'boasts great things' is translated by REB as *its pretensions are great,* which suggests that James is being scornful or dismissive of the tongue's claims. It is more likely that he is simply stating what he believes to be the case; if the tongue is capable of wreaking the havoc which the following verses describe, then it does indeed have much to boast about, even though such boasting is hardly to its credit. The illustration that a *vast amount of timber can be set ablaze by the tiniest spark* confirms the point. Whether the writer is thinking of a forest fire, a brushwood fire which might have been more familiar in Palestine[7] or a stack of timber, matters little. As anyone who has witnessed a major fire at first hand will confirm, the picture is a vivid one; the consequences often appear to be out of all proportion to the possible causes.

3.6   Most commentators understandably despair of making sense of this verse, at least in any great detail. Its grammatical structure is difficult to determine, its punctuation uncertain and the meaning of two of its most important phrases is disputed! That these problems were recognized early on is attested by the existence of variant readings in some Greek mss, and it is possible that the text has become corrupt. However, the REB translators produce reasonable sense, and we need not resort to amending the text unless we can make no sense of it except by doing so. *And the tongue is a fire* is fairly straightforward, concentrating, as in the previous verse, on the destructive nature of the fire, and therefore of the tongue. But what does it mean to say, *representing in our body the whole wicked world*? The phrase *whole wicked world* includes the Greek word *kosmos,* which James has already used in 1.27 and 2.5. There, as we have seen, it stands for that disposition in human nature and life which is antagonistic to God and to God's purposes. It seems likely that it also means that here. If so, the thought is probably that the tongue, because of its destructive capacities, is the 'enemy within'. It does more than symbolize the unrighteous world, it is an active agent of that world, *representing* it (in an active sense, as an Ambassador represents her country) in the body, which by right belongs to God. As one writer puts it, the tongue is 'a ready tool at the disposal of God's enemy, the ruler of this world'.[8] As such, it *pollutes our whole being*, perhaps in the sense that what we say, sinfully and too readily, expresses what is really in our hearts and minds. James has already said that 'pure and faultless religion' keeps itself *un*polluted by the world (1.27, REB 'untarnished'). Here the active agent of the pollution is tracked down; it is the tongue. Furthermore, *it sets the whole course of our existence alight*. The difficulties of the phrase translated 'whole course of our existence' can be seen from the way the different versions render it: 'course of nature' (AV); 'wheel of nature' (RV); 'cycle of nature' (RSV/NRSV); 'wheel of birth' (RSV/NRSVmg); 'wheel of our existence' (NEB); 'entire course of our existence' (GNB'); 'whole wheel of creation' (JB/NJB); 'whole course of his life' (NIV). It seems to have originated in the Orphic literature of ancient Greece, there meaning something like 'cycle of rebirth', which is probably a reference to a doctrine of reincarnation where souls transferred from one body to another as part of the unending pattern mapped out for them by fate. It is impossible to suppose that anything like that is in mind here. Almost all commentators support Dibelius' view that by the time of this epistle the original technical meaning had been lost and it had become a familiar expression for the ups and downs of life, 'much as the expression 'struggle for existence' which belongs to Darwinian language, may cause us to think of general social situations rather than specific relationships involving the laws of nature.'[9] S. Laws also valuably draws attention to its use in rabbinic literature: 'There is an ever rotating wheel in this world, and he who is rich today may not be so tomorrow, and he who is poor today may not be so tomorrow,' which certainly illustrates how such Hellenistic phrases had become part of the linguistic currency of Palestinian Judaism.[10] In the light of this, the REB translation almost certainly gives the correct sense. James is saying that the whole of our daily living is set ablaze by the tongue. Each and every human experience can be spoiled by what the tongue may do.

The final phrase of this verse is no less vivid: *its flames are fed by hell.* The *hell* which is meant is 'Gehenna', the Valley of the Sons of Hinnom to the south and west of Jerusalem. It came to be thought of as a place of burning, either because it was used for sacrificing children to the god Moloch before the practice was stopped by King Josiah (II Kings 23.10), or because it was re-named 'Valley of Slaughter' by Jeremiah when predicting punishment on the nation for its evil ways (Jer. 19.1–13). It is often claimed that following the return from exile, it served the inhabitants of Jerusalem as a refuse dump and incinerator, so the expression came to be used figuratively for the place of punishment. Whether or not that is so, by the time of Jesus it could be used figuratively, to describe the place of punishment in the next life (Matt. 5.22,29; 18.9; 23.15). Some assert that by this time it had also come to be believed that Satan, the prince of hell, had an existence there; but the evidence for this is less than certain. At any rate, the general thrust of the statement is perfectly clear: the tongue's evil activities are fed straight from hell itself. Human beings ought not to imagine it is a small matter to wrestle with the sins and temptations of the tongue: they have considerable power.

3.7   In referring to *beasts and birds* along with creatures that *crawl on the ground or swim in the sea* the writer puts us in mind of the OT passages which record how God made all such creatures intending that humans should 'have dominion' over them (Gen. 1.26,28). James' point is that human beings have indeed attained that degree of control over the animal creation. Most translations say that human beings have 'tamed' the wild animals, but that is unfortunate, suggesting the meaning 'domesticate'. REB's *subdued* is better; the illustration concerns the way in which the human creation has dominated the rest and pressed it into service (including, in many cases, its use for human food). Our author is not concerned with a proper interpretation of what it means to say that God has given humans 'dominion' in this way. Nor are twentieth-century worries about how such teaching relates to our need to act responsibly in an ecological sense anywhere in his mind. His point is simply that as a matter of fact, humans have achieved such dominance. The verse is marked by the use of catchwords, and we could properly translate: 'Beasts and birds of every kind . . . have been subdued by humankind.' There is an intended contrast with what follows.

3.8   *But no one can subdue the tongue.* The Greek is crisper and more emphatic: 'but the tongue . . .' – well, that is another story. There is an unusual word order here: 'But the tongue no one can subdue of men'; the last two words are added for emphasis so the phrase means 'no human being at all'. It has already been suggested that anyone who could subdue the tongue would thereby show perfection (v.2). St Augustine proffered an interpretation of a different kind: 'he does not say that no one can tame the tongue, but no one of men; so that when it is tamed we confess that this is brought about by . . . the grace of God.'[11] The thought is undoubtedly true and it is very much a preacher's point; unfortunately it is almost certainly not in James' mind! No human being is able to subdue the tongue because it is *an evil thing, restless and charged with deadly venom.* REB's *restless* might give the impression that the writer has in mind those who are unable to stop their tongues wagging, or who cannot stop talking. This however, is only part of the meaning. The same word is used in 1.8 where REB translates 'unstable'; here 'unreliable' or 'disorderly' seems called for. Yet the tongue is charged with worse than that, for it is full of *deadly venom.* The snake imagery is vivid and appropriate, even if a snake's venom comes through its fangs rather than through the flickering tongue which is such a notable feature of its appearance. The writer of Ps. 140.3 makes the point with reference to those bent on wicked schemes and with stirring up bitter strife: 'Their tongues are as deadly as serpents' fangs.' It might be felt that James (who so far has had nothing good to say about the tongue) is rather overdoing things. Possibly he is, but perhaps he needs to. There is sometimes a curious lack of awareness in Christian communities that the wrong use of the tongue is a sin at all. Whereas, for example, physical violence or theft amongst members would be immediately recognized as wrong, gossip, rumour and even downright nastiness in speech can become almost taken for granted. Yet few things so quickly destroy a Christian congregation's capacity to display the winsomeness of the gospel. Here too, the human capacity for self-deception must not be underestimated. What we deem rudeness in others we characterize as plain speaking in ourselves. The preacher who delivers a sermon on this passage might well expect to have someone say afterwards, 'That was a very good sermon. I'm only sorry so-and-so was not present to hear it.' We should recall too, that James began this section by referring to Christian teachers. Here, as so often, Bengel's dictum about studying the Bible is pertinent: 'Apply yourself wholly to the text; apply the text wholly to yourself.'

3.9 This verse seems to qualify the description of the tongue which the writer has so far offered, in which it appears as an unmitigated evil. *We use it to praise our Lord and Father*, he says, so perhaps there is something good to be said for it after all. *Lord and Father* is an unusual phrase, though not dissimilar to the one used in 1.27, where REB has 'God the Father'. That is what is meant here, and no direct reference to Jesus is intended. James has in mind the one true God of the OT revelation, now understood in the light of Jesus' teaching about him as our heavenly Father. When he refers to the way in which *praise* is offered to God, he reflects the way in which the praises of God are at the heart of worship in the Jewish and Christian traditions alike. Commentators quite properly refer to the famous 'Eighteen Benedictions', each beginning 'Blessed art thou, O Lord our God', provided for daily liturgical recitation by the devout Jew. It is however, important to realize that such praises of God are not confined in the Jewish tradition, then or now, to specific liturgical occasions. Benedictions beginning in the same way are provided for use on many occasions, from the taking of various kinds of food to 'hearing evil tidings'.[12] The point of this is that the blessing or praising of God is intended to be a constant activity, sanctifying the whole of human existence. Even experiences which might be considered strange or difficult are to be made an occasion for blessing God. Something of this can be sensed in those Psalms where the praise of God is central to the writer's concern. Most of them do not seem to have been written for cultic occasions, but the solemnity with which they offer their praise suggests that it was thought of as more than mere lip-service. To praise God in this way is for the worshipper an acknowledgement of indebtedness to, and dependence upon God, in every aspect of life.[13] Given this, the use of the tongue to *praise* God must certainly be considered the highest and purest function it can ever achieve. By such praises human life is consciously brought into relationship with the God who created it and intended it for good. James and his fellow-Christians would have had all this 'in their bones' so to say. The offering of such praises would have been part of the worship experience in their Jewish Christian synagogues, as well as of their daily lives. The tongue is clearly capable of such exalted use, but *then we use it to invoke curses on our fellow-men*. By so doing, all the good which has been achieved in the praising of God, is nullified or destroyed. Such use can surely only indicate that the praises of God were never genuinely intended to have their proper purpose of sanctifying life; amounted, in fact, to little more than hypocrisy. *Curses* are the exact opposite of blessings or praises. They are not mere idle swear words or expressions of irritation ('Oh, bother the man!'), nor legitimate criticisms of the actions of others. They are abusive, injurious and angry words directed at, or about, other people. As such they are clearly wrong in themselves, since they promote neither human happiness nor well-being. The writer also provides an additional theological reason for their unacceptability: those on whom we invoke such curses *are made in God's likeness* – just as we, who engage in the cursing are also made in God's likeness. The reference to Gen. 1.26 is surely intentional, not least because that text has already been alluded to in v.7. If all have been made in God's image, then the brotherly and sisterly bond which that fact itself provides should be a deterrent to the kind of cursing portrayed here. That it is not, is an illustration in itself of the tongue's propensity for evil – in fact that its flames are fed by hell (v.6). We should note that James seems to include himself amongst those who misuse their tongues in this way. This has caused some commentators disquiet, and led to the suggestion that by 'we' he means human being in general, or else is simply identifying with his audience. Yet the most natural way to understand this is that he does indeed include himself. After all, he has already stated that 'all of us go wrong' in this respect (v.2). The Christian teacher or pastor who makes the assumption that he or she has fewer or less blameworthy sins than the congregation is unlikely to be heard with respect.

3.10 The praises and curses come *out of the same mouth* (a slight change from the imagery of the 'tongue'). *This should not be so*; which is to say, such an occurrence is entirely unfitting. James has already told us that the person who is 'always in two minds' is unstable, a waverer, unable to decide whether to serve God or not (see the commentary on 1.8). This double-minded/heartedness is also shown by the quite incompatible words which come out of the same mouth. Our speech is to be taken seriously, as an indication of what is in our hearts (Matt. 15.18–20). Therefore, there is a need to pray, as in the ancient words of the Liturgy of Malabar, that acts of praise may result in lives which are lived in accordance with them:

Lord, may the tongues which 'Holy' sang
keep free from all deceiving. (*Hymns and Psalms* 626)

3.11 The illustration in this verse is put in the form of a question which expects the answer 'no'. The *fountain* is to be understood as a vigorous natural spring, not something artificially constructed; *fresh and brackish* is literally 'sweet and bitter', absolute opposites. The point of the illustration is not that both fresh and brackish water is found (in Palestine or anywhere else) in adjacent springs, but that you do not expect both *from the same outlet*. One spring may produce water which is fit for human consumption and a nearby one water which cannot be drunk, but they are two different springs. If a spring which normally produced good water suddenly produced water which was unusable, contamination would properly be suspected. Moreover, the unreliability of such a source in a country where fresh water is in short supply would be a serious matter. It is, of course, not normally expected, which is James' point. Springs usually continue to produce water of the kind they have always produced. Human speech, by contrast, produces first good things, and then bad.

3.12 The illustration that plants produce only what they are genetically programmed to produce, as we might express it today, is often said to have been fairly widespread in Greek literature, especially in the writings of the Stoics. If James is using an illustration culled from this source, then once again he is not quite at ease with it. The point about the mouth in v.10 and the spring in v.11 is concerned with consistency and reliability. We might therefore have expected this illustration to have been:' Does a fig tree produce figs on some occasions but olives on others?' whereas what he actually says points to the reliability of what each plant produces and the irrationality of expecting anything else. The illustration may remind us of the sayings of Jesus about good and bad trees always yielding the only kind of fruit they are capable of producing (Matt. 7.16–18; 12.33). Yet the point is not exactly the same, for Jesus was referring to good and bad characters showing themselves in corresponding deeds. However, in this connection Jesus is recorded as asking the question: 'How can your words be good when you yourselves are evil?' (Matt. 12.34), which is somewhat closer to what James says here, inasmuch as he has argued that the bad results of the tongue indicate its alliance with evil (v.6). It may well be that the sayings of Jesus concerning good and bad plants/people were known to James but in a somewhat earlier form than that in which they are now recorded in the synoptic gospels. We cannot be sure of this, but the links are unlikely to be totally coincidental. The concluding statement, *No more can salt water produce fresh* is, in detail at least, something of a puzzle, though its main thrust is clear. A source of salty water, whether a lake (as the Dead Sea), or a spring, cannot suddenly produce water of a different kind. As in the other illustrations, in various ways, the end result must be consistent with the starting-point. So far as James' teaching on Christian speaking is concerned, the point is as it has been all along: the way in which we use our tongues reveals what is within our characters. All too often that is formed not as it should be, by the 'word of truth' (1.18), but by the influence of evil to which the tongue gives entry. In the next section of the epistle the writer reflects on some of the practical consequences of this.

The sin of envy
3.13–4.12

This section has often been viewed as little more than a loosely arranged collection of moral sayings, bearing no real relationship to what goes before or comes after it. Such a judgement misses the unity which is imparted (at least as far as 4.10) by the related themes of jealousy and selfishness. These themes are discussed in general terms in 3.13–18, with more specific reference to problems within the community in 4.1–6, and rounded off by a call to repentance and a changed way of life in 4.7–10. Jealousy and selfishness are contrasted with the need for true wisdom which is the gift of God. This is an unpacking of the theme announced in the 'contents list' at 1.5 and 1.17. However, it does not do this quite as neatly as we have observed with previous sections, and we must beware of trying to fit it into a predetermined structure. There are close resemblances to earlier Jewish writings, in particular the *Testaments of the Twelve Patriarchs*. The date and provenance of those writings is a difficult matter anyway, and there is no evidence that James is directly dependent on them. It has also been argued that the author is here utilizing a pattern of moral exhortation familiar in the Hellenistic literature, a *topos* on envy.[1] There may be some truth in that, though, as we shall argue, this cannot be taken to mean that James has no concrete situation within the church in his mind.

3.13 *Which of you is wise or learned*? has sometimes been interpreted with reference to 3.1, as if James has teachers specifically in view. No doubt teachers are included, but others are also in mind. The question is directed towards self-examination, posing a challenge. In I Cor. 1.20 Paul puts a question which has a superficial similarity to this one, but the contexts are quite different. Whereas Paul contrasts the wisdom of God with the wisdom of the 'present age', James is characteristically concerned with whether those who think of themselves as possessing wisdom and understanding can give *practical proof* of it. Such wisdom, which is the ability to lead one's life in the way God requires, and to walk in the way of the gospel, is open to all Christians, indeed expected of them. Those who are aware of their lack of wisdom are invited to pray for it, and assured that if they ask in faith they will receive it (1.5). In the same way that merely claiming to have faith, but with no actions to prove that the claim is realistic, will not do (2.14ff.), so neither will a claim to possess wisdom and understanding be of any use unless it can be demonstrated in *right conduct*. What if someone says: 'Well, I am certainly wise; you only have to look at the way I conduct my life to see that'? Such an attitude would be very close to those who paraded their religion before others and were condemned by Jesus for doing so (Matt. 6.1ff.). It is therefore necessary to remind the readers that true *wisdom* produces *modesty*. This is the quality of 'meekness' already referred to at 1.21 in a different context, here meaning humility or gentleness. James draws upon his Jewish background; humility was a quality not much prized by pagan writers, who equated it with subservience and weakness. It is neither of those things, but 'strength under control'[2] shown in the ability not to boast about the gifts one has been given.

3.14   If the possession of true wisdom is shown by right conduct, then wrong conduct must demonstrate that such wisdom is absent. What is this wrong conduct which James condemns? REB's *jealousy* is a rather one-sided translation of the Greek word (*zēlos*), which can have both good and bad meanings. In Acts 22.3 Paul uses it to describe his attitude, prior to his Damascus road experience, towards the faith of his ancestors (see Gal.1.14). Such boundless devotion and ardour seemed to him at the time entirely commendable, but with hindsight can be seen to have been misdirected, leading as it did to his persecution of the followers of Jesus. Zeal is in itself a neutral quality: whether it becomes good or bad depends partly on its objectives and partly on the way it is put into practice. Where it turns to fanaticism there is an ever-present danger that hatred, directed towards those who do not share the fanatic's viewpoint, will follow. In II Cor. 12.20 this vice is linked with 'quarrelling and angry tempers', which also suggests the element of personal animosity. It is impossible to be absolutely sure which of these senses James primarily intends. Perhaps they are so closely linked that separating them is impossible. He goes on to condemn *the spirit of rivalry* (which is a better rendition than NIV's 'selfish ambition' or

GNB's 'selfishness'). In this context it refers to party spirit, of the kind which produced divisions within the church in Corinth (I Cor. 1.10–12, though Paul does not use the same word in this connection). The presence of such jealousy and rivalry within the congregation indicates that people are not living in harmony with each other, but allowing their own vested interests (whether concerning some matter of doctrine or practice, or involving matters of a more personal kind) to take precedence.[3] Either way, God's wisdom is then not at work and the life of the community as a whole is not served. James therefore instructs: *stop making false claims in defiance of the truth*. To do so would, of course, be wrong in any event. It is demonstrably wrong when the claim is the possession of wisdom but the claimants are actually filled with rivalry and jealousy.

3.15   Whatever kind of wisdom people who behave like this imagine they possess, one thing is clear; it *is not the wisdom that comes from above*. The wisdom which forms part of the perfect gifts which 'come from above', is from God himself (1.17). As such it reflects the character of the giver who does not change and who, as Jesus said, gives good gifts to his children (Matt. 7.11). The kind of 'wisdom' claimed by people living in rivalry and factionalism however, can only be described in terms which denote its real origin. It is *earthbound*, a term which is neutral in itself, but in this kind of context means 'earthly' as opposed to 'heavenly'. It is also *sensual*, which is a more difficult term. The Greek word (*psychikos*) is only found elsewhere in the NT in I Cor. (2.14; 15.44,46), where REB translates 'unspiritual' for the first occurrence and 'physical' for the others, and at Jude 19, where REB again has 'unspiritual'. When Paul uses it he probably means 'natural', though we must bear in mind that in his theological scheme, 'the purely natural, because of the Fall, is unnatural.'[4] The 'natural' person then, is one who has not received the Spirit and for this reason cannot understand the things of God. This also seems to be the use in Jude 19, where the writer is complaining about those who have no understanding of spiritual realities, though they claim that they do. How far we can deduce the meaning of the word in this epistle from its use by Jude and Paul is another matter, because both those writers are dealing with opponents who follow false teachings, and this does not seem to be the situation in James. However, the meaning of 'unspiritual' in the sense of not being directed by the Spirit fits the context, not least because our writer will later refer to the 'spirit which God implanted in us' (4.5). The third term which describes this so-called wisdom is *demonic*. This is a highly unusual adjective, not found anywhere else in the NT, which may refer to either the nature or the source of such 'wisdom'. The latter is more likely, because James will later include in his call to repentance the instruction, 'stand up to the devil' (4.7). However we interpret the precise details of this verse, the thrust is straight-forward enough: those whose lives are dominated by jealousy and rivalry may claim to be spiritual, to have their lives under God's direction, but their conduct suggests the exact opposite.

3.16   Let no one imagine that all this is a matter of abstract specula-tion: it matters very much whether Christians are living by true or false wisdom. If the latter, then *disorder* will follow. Disorder in the church is a serious problem and Paul, dealing with it in another con-text, enunciated the underlying theological principle that 'God is not a God of disorder but of peace' (I Cor. 14.33). James does much the same thing here, by contrasting the 'wisdom' which produces such disorder with the true wisdom which comes from God above (v.15). Worse even than such disorder, living by false wisdom produces *the practice of every kind of evil*, which seems a bit sweeping, but perhaps it is not too strong to describe forces which can tear apart a Christian congregation, undermining both its fellowship and its witness to the gospel.

3.17   *But* introduces us to the contrast, which is strong and deliberate. The *wisdom from above*, reflecting the character of the giver, is *in the first place pure*. The word (Gk. *hagnē*) is used to denote sexual purity (II Cor. 11.2; I Peter 3.2), but it is also used at I John 3.3, where the writer refers to the time when we shall see Christ as he is and adds, 'as he is pure, everyone who has grasped this hope makes himself pure.' The basic sense is of being without moral blemish or fault. This wisdom which comes from God partakes of God's own moral purity and, as such, cannot give rise to the evil and sinful consequences which have already been described. James proceeds to expand the nature of this pure wisdom in a series of adjectives describing the virtues, as he has previously described the vices. It is *peace-loving*, in contrast to the disputatious nature of the false wisdom. Such a peace is not like a truce, a situation in which conflict happens to be absent or has been suspended. It is *shalom*, a deep desire for harmony and well-being within relationships. God's wisdom is also *considerate*, which is the REB's translation of 'gentle' –

a Christlike quality to which Paul appeals in II Cor. 10.1. In the context of relationships with others, *considerate* is indeed what it means, since this virtue does not demand its own way. God's wisdom is also *open-minded*, REB's helpful translation of another Greek word unique to James in the New Testament. It has the sense of 'persuadable', even 'trusting', which would not have been recognized as a virtue by the zealots of v.14, any more than it is always recognized as one by Christian people who hold strong views today. But how is it possible to have a community which is peace-loving and considerate, unless this virtue is also valued and practised? It does not mean that we must be moved around by every shift of fashionable opinion, but it does mean that we should ask ourselves more often than perhaps we do, whether the fellow-Christian with whom we disagree might not sometimes be right! At the very least it means granting others the sincerity and integrity of their views. This easily-overlooked virtue becomes all the more important when the church is deeply divided over some matter of ethics or practice. James says that it is one of the characteristics of the wisdom of God. Another is that it is *straightforward*, a word peculiar to James, whose precise meaning is hard to pin down. Related words are found at 1.6 and 2.4, where they are opposed to doubting and discriminating, so the meanings 'dependable' and 'impartial' are possibilities here. *Straightforward* is a good translation, suggesting as it does the person whose judgement, whilst considerate and open-minded, will not be swayed by threats or promises and who is not, as we say, 'in anyone's pocket'. With this is coupled the quality of being *sincere*, without pretence and hypocrisy. This is how Paul tells us Christian love should be (Rom. 12.9). The wisdom of God is also *rich in compassion*, reminding us that mercy and compassion are at the heart of God's relationship to us and should therefore characterize our relationships with one another (Matt. 18.23ff.). Finally, it is rich in *deeds of kindness*, which reminds us of James' insistence that compassion should be shown in action (2.14–16). Such loving concern is now said to be the *fruit* of God's wisdom. Although there are few similarities in vocabulary, it is almost impossible not to be reminded of the list of virtues which Paul describes as the 'fruit of the Spirit' (Gal. 5.22–23). It is striking that Paul says the *Spirit* produces such qualities in the lives of believers, and that James says God's *wisdom* does so. There is also the significant fact that in both Paul and James, these qualities stand in opposition to that which is 'unspiritual' (Gal.5.19; James 3.15; see also the comments on 'earthbound' in v.15). The Epistle of James has no direct references to the Spirit (unless we count 4.5, which is doubtful), and this has led some scholars to suggest that when James uses the concept of God's wisdom, as here, he is expressing what Paul and others express elsewhere by means of the concept of the Holy Spirit.[5] This would fit well with the overall sense in James of wisdom as a divine quality, 'from above' and sharing the character of the Father who is the giver (1.17).

3.18   The quality of peace, which previously figured as the first characteristic of the pure wisdom of God, now returns. There is no other obvious link between vv. 17 and 18, and for this reason some commentators think it a proverbial or independent saying, which James or his editor has added at this point. It has been argued that James has in mind the reference to Prov. 3.18, where it is said that wisdom is a 'tree of life to those who grasp her', and that he views wisdom as the 'fruit of righteousness'.[6] It is true that this author sometimes uses the OT writings in this kind of allusive way, but this connection seems altogether too remote to be helpful. Two things are particularly interesting about this verse. In the first place, as C. L. Mitton sees, James reverses what is usually regarded as the natural order of things.[7] He writes that *peace is the seed-bed of righteousness*, or in the even more vivid rendering of NJB, 'The peace sown by peacemakers brings a harvest of justice'. Usually in the OT, it is the other way round; justice and righteousness produce the conditions in which peace can flourish. Mitton rightly refers to Isa. 32.17 as the epitome of this viewpoint: 'righteousness will yield peace and bring about quiet trust for ever.' This has also become a commonplace in twentieth-century thinking about justice and peace. We are conscious that, like those condemned by Jeremiah, Christians have often been too willing to say '"Peace, peace" . . . when there is no peace' (Jer. 6.14, NIV). When Christians have done this they have often colluded with, or turned a blind eye to, the actions of unjust and oppressive regimes. Therefore, we say, true peace can only be achieved when just and fair dealings have been established; otherwise we are failing to deal with underlying causes. The value of this insight seems undeniable, yet it is not what James says here. Is he simply wrong, or is there something to be said for his point of view? Here the second interesting thing about this verse comes into the picture. There is a reasonable amount of exhortation in the NT writings about being at peace or living in peace with others, but only one other NT text speaks of peace*makers* and that is, of course,

Matt. 5.9, where such people are commended by Jesus and told that they will be called children of God. It is not those who seek peace in the sense of smoothing over difficulties and keeping things quiet at any cost who are commended by James, but those who seek to *create* genuine peace. And how can that be done, except by, amongst other things, searching out the root causes of conflicts, the injustices which lie behind tense and violent situations, and seeking to remedy them? James has already said in 1.20 that God's righteousness is not promoted by human violence; now he says that neither can righteousness in relationships between human beings be promoted by violence. Those who seek genuinely right and just human relationships will use the means appropriate to their cause, that is, peaceable ones. In thus making peace they do indeed plant *the seed-bed of righteousness* and they, though not they alone, *will reap its harvest.*

4.1–2 *What causes fighting and quarrels among you*? The literal meaning of these two Greek words is well represented by NJB, 'wars and battles', but some translations understand them, as here, in a somewhat softened, even metaphorical way. This is certainly possible with *quarrels* (Gr. *machai*), since the word is used in that way at II Cor. 7.5; II Tim. 2.23 and Tit. 3.9. It is less easy to see how *fighting* (Gr. *polemoi*) can be used metaphorically, since it has a militaristic sense in all the twelve other NT occurrences, half of which come in the Book of Revelation to describe various apocalyptic battles which will take place before the end. Given what has been said about the evils of the tongue (3.1–12) and the danger of disorder and evil practice (3.16), such a sense is not impossible, especially if James intends the two words to be more or less synonymous. If an actual situation is in view here, then whether real violence had broken out in the community is an arguable point, but antagonisms, feuds, verbal arguments and deep disagreements are certainly envisaged. It is possible that an actual situation *is* in view, for the writing takes on a new urgency and a more personal note in these verses. In 3. 13–18 the writer is certainly describing evils within the church, but in somewhat generalized terms: *if* the readers are harbouring bitter jealousy (v.14), then dire consequences will follow. Here however, the quarrels and fightings are *among you*, and they ought not to be. Their cause, or origin, must be sought in *the appetites that war in your bodies.* We are reminded of 1.14, though the vocabulary is now different. The *appetites* can hardly be purely sensual ones – though the word is *hēdonai*, from which we get 'hedonism', meaning the unrestricted pursuit of pleasure. It is used in this sense in Tit. 3.3, but here it means 'desires' or 'passions' in the wider sense; all those impulses and ambitions within human beings which seek gratification, perhaps at the expense of others. They appear in many guises: people can have *appetites* not only for the 'good things of life', for sex or for money, but also for fame, reputation, status and power. Even deep passions for that which seems altruistic, perhaps some political programme or moral crusade, may take on the temper of fanaticism and rivalry (3.14), so losing its altruistic quality and becoming essentially selfish. Such desires, the readers are told, *war in your bodies*. It is just possible that *bodies* refers to the members of the community, so that James has in mind the way in which such desires cause friction between people. More probably however, it means something like 'inside yourselves'. Each person who engages in fighting and quarrels, does so because he or she is not wholly directed by God, but inwardly torn and divided. James has already depicted such a situation in 1. 6–8. Those who have a divided loyalty and are not at peace with themselves cannot live at peace with others.

Various suggestions have been made regarding how v.2 should be punctuated. It is best to take it as in REB; two statements, each followed by a consequence. The first is: *You want what you cannot have, so you murder*. The mention of murder is somewhat startling. It causes such obvious difficulties that some have suggested emending the text, reading the Greek word for 'you envy' (*phthoneite*) instead of 'you murder/kill' (*phoneuete*). In favour of this it can be said that it makes sense in the context. Also, a small minority of mss of Gal. 5.21 do in fact read 'murder' instead of 'envy', and an even smaller number of mss of I Peter 2.1 do the same, showing that it was possible for copyists to confuse these two words. Against this suggestion however, is the decisive fact that not a single ms of the Epistle of James has 'envy' at this point. The emendation, however tempting, is wholly conjectural and must be rejected. Yet can we possibly envisage circumstances in which the readers are engaged in killing? 0r do we not need to do so?

One way out of the difficulty is to spiritualize the meaning of 'murder/kill' in this verse, on the analogy with 5.6, where James accuses the rich of condemning and murdering 'the innocent one'. In that passage he appears to be using 'murder' as a forceful expression to denote the effective outcome of the policy of oppression pursued by the rich. However, 5.6 is not helpful here, because (a) it is addressed to those outside the Christian community, whereas this verse is equally clearly addressed to those inside and (b) although many vices appear in the context of the present passage, they do not include oppression, whether by the rich or anyone else. Another approach is to recognize that in the Hellenistic writings, those who dealt with the theme of envy, as James does in this passage, frequently made the connection between envy and murder.[8] In such writings envy is viewed as antisocial and one of the root causes of violence. On this understanding, by employing this well-worn pattern of teaching James is reminding his readers of the known connections between envy and killing. In this case he is saying in effect: 'You know what happens when you give way to bitter envy – it will end in murder.' A similar thought is found in the teaching of Jesus (Matt. 5.21–30).[9] This may be so, but such an interpretation does not account for the sense we have that maybe envy/hatred already *has* ended in murder, and so we are left with the question whether we can envisage any circumstances in which the readers might be facing this accusation in reality, rather than as a hypothetical outcome of their attitudes. Any suggestion along these lines must, in the nature of the case, be somewhat speculative. However, we might remember that James is writing at a time when Jewish nationalist feeling was running high. It is not inconceivable that some Jewish Christians had become involved in those groups often described by the catch-all title of 'Zealot'[10] whose policy of opposition to Roman rule included the murder of leading Roman officials and those who collaborated with them. The widespread view that the whole of the first seven decades of the first century AD was marked by political instability and widespread Zealot activity needs some revision.[11] Nevertheless, the instability in Palestine increased from about AD 46 onwards, which fits with our understanding of the setting of the Epistle of James (see the Introduction: 'Life-setting, date and authorship'). To be involved in such activities would have been regarded in some quarters as honourable; a true form of Jewish patriotism in which God's sovereignty was identified with the sovereignty of the people of God and associated with the goal of political liberty.[12] If some of the readers had become involved with nationalist groups of this kind, they would be guilty of complicity and association with murder, even if their own hands had not wielded the dagger. James might well have regarded this as an example of honest aspirations which had become fanatical and thus an example of the wrong kind of 'wisdom' (3.14–15). The disciples of Jesus, both before and after the resurrection, included both Simon the Zealot (Luke 6.15/Acts 1.13) and Matthew the tax-collector, who worked for the Romans (Matt. 9.9/Acts 1.13), so there would be a continuing concern for how Jewish Christians related to such nationalist aspirations. It is at least possible that James is here reminding them that violence and *murder* and association with organizations which engage in them, are incompatible with the way of God's wisdom.[13] This would also go some way to explaining the emphasis on peace and peace-making in 3.18, which does not seem to spring very directly from the preceding verses. If however, 3.18 is taken to introduce 4.1, it fits much better. This interpretation also allows us to take the two words for 'wars' and 'battles', both here and in v.1, in a sense which more nearly approaches their natural meaning.

It is because they passionately desire something, yet are unable to attain their *ambition* to possess it (whether it be satisfaction of an immediate personal need or ambition of some other kind), that they – James repeats – *quarrel and fight*. This failure to achieve their ambition is ascribed to the fact that they *do not pray for it*. Taken on its own this is an odd remark, because what would be the use of praying for ambitions which the writer regards as unworthy? Or is it not so much the ambitions themselves as the methods of achieving them which are unworthy? In any event, the statement is immediately qualified.

4.3   Even if the readers do pray for what they want, their *requests are not granted*, and this is because of the *wrong motives* of such prayers. Properly instructed Christians have never believed that any and every request made in prayer will be granted. Even Matt. 7.7, which appears to read in this way, contains hints that such prayer has to be for things which are worthwhile in themselves, as the language of seeking and finding and of the opening of doors suggests. In the Fourth Gospel, Jesus teaches his disciples to ask in his name (John 14.13) and that is neither a simple liturgical formula nor an invitation to demand anything one pleases but, 'a promise to honour requests of a believer who hopes to demonstrate the glory of God in Jesus'.[14] So here: if the asking and acting were genuinely in the name of Jesus that would be one thing, but far from that, it is in order that God's bounty may be wasted on *pleasures* (not just sensual pleasures, as we have seen; better 'to indulge your passions' NJB).

4.4 *Unfaithful creatures*! obscures an interesting point in the Greek, as do most other translations (e.g., GNB, 'unfaithful people'; NIV, 'adulterous people'; NJB, 'adulterers'). The word James uses is feminine, and literally means 'adulteresses' (Gr. *moichalides*). Why does James use a feminine term to address readers who are everywhere else addressed in masculine grammatical terms? J. J. Schmitt has very persuasively argued that the writer has a specific biblical text in mind, namely Prov. 30.20.[15] In the Hebrew text it contains a vivid picture of an adulteress: 'she eats, then wipes her mouth and says, "I have done nothing wrong."' The LXX version is if anything, even more striking: 'who, having washed herself from what she has done, says she has done nothing unnatural.' She is not only an adulteress, but an unrepentant one who can see nothing wrong in her actions. If James does have this picture at the back of his mind, he may intend to suggest to his readers that they have lost the moral sensitivity which should characterize a friend of God. Sexual sins are not in mind here; this is a metaphor for unfaithfulness to God, as REB recognizes, though a more interesting one than might have been at first supposed. Why are the readers unfaithful to God? Because they should know that by choosing to be friends with *the world* they put themselves in *enmity to God*. James has used *the world* three times already in his epistle, and its occurrence at 1.27 is the important parallel. Here, as there, it is not a disdainful reference to human culture as such, nor a condemnation of social structures in themselves, but a description of human life and society as it is organized in opposition to God and in ignorance of God's wisdom. Societies may be more, or less, open to God's purposes, depending on the extent to which they are permeated by the kingdom values which the followers of Jesus have been able to bring to bear on them. But in so far as society operates wholly or partly in opposition to those values it is 'worldly'. Here *the world* refers to those values which are totally opposed to God's purposes for human life. What then, does it mean to be the *world's friend*? Given the high regard for friendship in the Greek world, and the view that it involved a spiritual relationship of shared values and perceptions, such a description can only mean that one has come to share, in a quite intimate way, the understanding of those opposed to God. The person who chooses such a course naturally becomes *God's enemy* (in distinction to Abraham, who by accepting God's call to obedience and acting on it made himself 'God's friend', 2.23).[16]

4.5   We are now given a supporting argument for what has just been said, but it is one of the most difficult verses in the epistle. The first and most obvious difficulty is that James appears to appeal to *scripture*, either by way of direct citation (so RSV,NRSV,GNB,NJB) or allusion (so RV,NEB,JB?,NIV,REB). This *scripture* says: *the spirit which God implanted in us is filled with envious longings*, and there is no such statement in the OT, at least in any of its known texts or versions, or for that matter, in any other writing. It is therefore often thought to be from a book which is now entirely lost to us and, if that is the case, there is no point in speculating on which book that might have been. A second difficulty is knowing exactly how the verse should be punctuated. One of the most recent attempts to cut this particular Gordian knot is by S. Laws[17] who argues for the following: 'Or do you think that scripture speaks to no effect? Does the spirit which he made to dwell in us long enviously?' Punctuating it thus, as two rhetorical questions, allows her to argue that the reference to the speaking of 'scripture' is not to a specific text, but to the general sense of a number of texts, particularly from Psalms. James, in other words, is arguing, 'the Bible says . . .' without specifying which part of the Bible he has in mind. This is a most attractive solution in many ways, but we are compelled to reject it on two grounds. Firstly, the formula 'scripture says' (Gr. *graphe legei*) normally (arguably, invariably) refers to the citation of a specific text. Secondly, even if this were not so, the general sense she suggests is just *too* allusive. If James intends his readers to understand such a general sense, he does not succeed; they would be quite justified in asking, '*Where* does scripture say this?', the very question which has been asked ever since. We are therefore forced to concede, however reluctantly, that we simply have no idea where James found his 'scripture'. This is not a unique instance, although it provides the most puzzling of the NT occurrences. There is uncertainty of one kind or another about the 'scriptural quotations' in Matt. 2.23, John 7.38, I Cor. 2.9, Eph. 5.14 and II Tim. 3.8.[18] Furthermore, the Epistle of Jude quotes from the apocalyptic book of I Enoch at vv.14–15 and possibly from a lost work at v.9. The use of the introductory formula in this way is also found in the literature from Qumran.[19] Perhaps at this period neither Jews nor Christians were as concerned as we sometimes are today, with the precise delimitation of their Bible!

If we could identify the original source of the quotation we would be some way towards understanding what it means, but that is not the case. It is not easy to decide whether it is a statement or a question, whether the subject is God or the 'spirit' and, if it is the 'spirit' whether James is referring to the Holy Spirit or the human spirit! RSV provides an unambiguous rendering in line with the view that the subject is God: 'He yearns jealously over the spirit which he has made to dwell in us.' This has the advantage that it is a clear supporting statement to what has been said in the previous verse; God wishes us to be his friends, not the friends of the 'world', and therefore he yearns jealously over the spirit he has made to dwell in us. The major objection to this, is that the word which RSV translates 'jealously' is normally translated as 'enviously', and has negative connotations referring to human sinfulness. It seems a very strange word to use about God. Commentators who support this translation point out that in 3.14,16, when James refers to sinful human jealousy he uses, not this word, but another (Gr. *zēlos* – see the commentary on 3.14). James might, therefore, choose a different word here to make the contrast plain.[20] This is not impossible, but it leaves the unsuitability of the actual word unexplained. REB provides us with a translation in line with the view that the subject is the spirit, here said to be *filled with envious longings*. In this case, the quotation is a warning that the human spirit is all too liable to corruption, easily filled with the kind of 'jealousy' which James has been condemning. No reference to the Holy Spirit can therefore be intended. This gives the word for 'envious' its usual negative meaning and does not require us to apply it to God, which is difficult. The argument that this translation does not follow on from the previous verse as a supporting statement is not as strong as is often claimed. The warning that making yourself the friend of the world thereby makes you God's enemy, can quite naturally be followed by the further warning that it is all too easy to indulge in such friendship with the world. The human spirit, though implanted by God, does not remain faithful to its intended purpose, but becomes seduced by the world's system of values. No solution to the problems of this difficult verse can be claimed as perfect, but REB offers us a translation which makes sense of the text and provides a good link (by way of a contrast) with the next verse.

4.6   *But the grace he gives is stronger*, must now mean that despite the corruptibility of the human spirit, the fallibility of human intentions and the ease with which people become friends with the world (all of which paint a rather depressing picture), there is no need for despair. God supplies *grace*, and this is stronger than all the evil impulses which would otherwise shape a human destiny, and can therefore overcome them. This simple statement sometimes seems difficult to believe. The pressures to live by the world's values (what 'everybody else' is alleged to do) rather than the values of the kingdom, can seem well-nigh irresistible at times. On the other side there is only grace; but grace is weak in the world's view. It does not demand, it offers; it does not compel, it invites. Yet, James tells us, in grace which is sought and received, there is something truly *stronger* than anything the world can offer. As it is expressed elsewhere, 'the weakness of God is stronger than human strength' (I Cor. 1.25). However, if this overcoming grace is to be received, the attitude of the seeker must be right; *thus scripture says, 'God opposes the arrogant and gives grace to the humble.'* This scriptural quotation is clear enough; it is from Prov. 3.34. Its meaning is also clear enough: the arrogant are those who do not recognize their need of God's grace, but are happy enough being friends of the world and determining their own way of life without reference to God. Those who are humble, by contrast, recognize their need to submit to God and thereby to walk in the way of true wisdom. This insistence on humble submission is developed in the following verses as James expands on the meaning of the biblical quotation.[21]

4.7–10 The writer now issues a series of commands (known as 'imperatives'), which when taken together, form a thoroughgoing demand for repentance against the background of the evils he has been describing, and for submission to the will of God. The parallels with I Peter 5.5–9 have often been noted, though they are not as close as is sometimes claimed and the context is quite different. Here, the basic command to the readers to *submit* and *humble* themselves begins the series in v.7 and concludes it in v.10, thus making it plain that it is the main theme of the verses. Elsewhere in the New Testament, only at Heb. 12.9 is there a command of this kind to submit to God; usually this word refers to submission to human authorities of various sorts (Rom. 13.1; Eph. 5.22; I Peter 2.13). Here it is obviously a call to the readers to bring their whole way of life under the will and direction of God. As Charles Wesley expresses it:

Not to man, but God submit,
Lay my reasonings at thy feet.   (*Hymns and Psalms* 737)

Between the opening and closing imperatives, there are three couplets which spell out the meaning of this requirement in more detail.

Firstly, *Stand up to the devil, and he will turn and run.*
Come close to God, and he will draw close to you

If twentieth-century Christians are hesitant about speaking of *the devil*, this may partly be due to an awareness that in many people's minds such terminology only conjures up a pantomime figure with horns and a tail who is not to be taken seriously. Yet the question of whether we have outgrown such language is not so easily settled. In the biblical tradition Satan ('the adversary') is translated by the Greek word *diabolos* ('devil') in the LXX, and the identification of the two is made plain in Rev. 20.2. The notion of a spiritual power in opposition to God is found in the gospels, where amongst other things, it is said to infiltrate the world in the present time (Matt. 13.39), to prevent people hearing the gospel (Mark 4.15), to be responsible for human disability (Luke 13.16), to have motivated Judas Iscariot in his act of betrayal (Luke 22.3) and to lose its power when work is done in the name of Jesus (Luke 10.18). Elsewhere, there is acknowledgment of the reality of such a spiritual power and of its danger to the Christian life (Eph. 4.27, 6.11; I Peter 5.8–9). The writer of the epistle undoubtedly believed in such a *devil*. Those who find this belief difficult to share, and who prefer to regard the terminology as a metaphor for the mystery of human evil, nevertheless need to recognize the emphasis here on the necessity of standing up to such evil. James has already said that temptation does not come from God, but from a person's own evil inclination (1.14–15). If he here in some sense traces that evil inclination back to its source, he nevertheless also emphasizes the individual's responsibility for personal response. The readers must resist the evil one and, when they do, can be confident that *he will turn and run* – a dramatic picture of the overcoming of temptation. The corollary of this, is that believers must *come close to God*. This process begins in the resistance to evil, but must be completed by a positive turning to God. God, the writer says, responds to such repentance by giving his presence.

Secondly, *Sinners, make your hands clean;*
you whose motives are mixed, see that your hearts are pure.

The notion of washing hands as a symbol of ritual purity is deeply embedded in OT practice (Exod. 30.19–21) and then came to be thought of in terms of moral purity as well. In Ps. 24.4, the person who may stand in the Lord's holy place is the one 'who has clean hands and a pure heart', there defined as the person who has nothing to do with falsehood and deceitfulness. It is necessary for the readers to purify themselves (morally, not ritually), because in engaging in the behaviour described in vv.1–4, they have contaminated themselves. We note here how James lays aside his usual form of address 'brothers'/'dear friends' to call them *sinners*. He also defines them as *you whose motives are mixed*, using the same rare word (Gr. *dipsuchos*) as he used at 1.8 to describe those 'in two minds'. As it is used in this context, it refers to those whose minds are not settled on whether they are to be the friends of God or the friends of the world (v.4). This undecidedness is itself proof that they are sinners who require repentance.

Thirdly, *Be sorrowful, mourn, and weep.*
Turn your laughter into mourning and your gaiety into gloom.

Mourning and weeping 'are the accompaniments of repentance, not the substitutes for it'.[22] There is nothing wrong with laughter and gaiety, indeed much that is right for those who know themselves to be the loved children of God and who intend to enjoy the life he has given them. But there are times when recognition of sin and error, of having seriously compromised oneself with the world's values, do not permit lighthearted brushing aside of what has happened. The repentance which is called for here is not merely wishing one had not done something because the consequences are unpleasant (as when someone suffering a hangover vows never to drink too much alcohol again), nor an emotional spasm caused by having been detected in wrongdoing. Rather, it is a recognition that one's way of life has become directed away from God and from God's will and purpose. Under these circumstances serious reflection and action is called for, and only re-orientation of that way of life will suffice. We hear this tone in the prophets (Joel 2.12–13; Amos 8.10) with the warning that the mourning and weeping is not enough if the sinful actions persist (Mal. 2.13–16). We hear it now from James as the proper accompaniment of genuine repentance.

The call to submit to God is not mere repetition. The need for, and the result of, repentance is now made plain, and set in the context of God's future judgement. The grace which God gives to the humble, mentioned in the quotation from Prov. 3.34 in v.6, now appears not just as supplying strength for the present, but also as a pledge of future salvation. Jesus's story of the tax-collector who went home justified concludes with the aphorism: 'For everyone who exalts himself will be humbled; and whoever humbles himself will be exalted' (Luke 18.14) and the same saying is found in two quite different contexts describing human behaviour (Matt. 23.12; Luke 14.11). James applies it in a different way here (though perhaps with overtones of the Lucan story), suggesting that those who are truly repentant will be exalted (i.e. saved) by God. Despite the tendency of the human spirit to become corrupted (v.5) and the evils which arise from the resultant passions and ambitions, God's grace is indeed stronger. Despair is not necessary; restoration and salvation follow genuine repentance because that is the nature of a God who is constant towards us (1.17).

4.11–12 These verses form a very short section on their own, having no obvious connection with what precedes or follows them. This looks very much like the work of an editorial hand, a reminder of a possible homiletic origin for much of the material in this epistle. Even so, there are other places where this passage might have fitted rather better, and its presence here is an oddity, not quite accounted for by the suggestion that some parallel NT passages exhibit many of the themes of 4.1–10.[23] It begins by reverting to the usual way in which the readers are addressed, and to the theme of Christian speaking, as it was announced in 1.19,26, and then developed in different ways in 2.12 and 3.1–12. Here however, James is specifically concerned with the way people *speak ill of one another* and should not. This is not quite the same as using the tongue to curse other people (3.9). The specific sin of slander is in mind: not so much speaking ill *to* someone (as in 3.9), but speaking ill *of* them, possibly with the implication that what is said is 'behind their backs'. Such behaviour is specifically forbidden by Lev. 19.16: 'Do not go about spreading slander among your father's kin,' and James may well have that specific text in mind, even though there is no specific verbal resemblance.[24] Slander is condemned elsewhere in the OT (Ps.50.20; Prov.30.11), and also occurs in the lists of those things which Christians are to avoid (II Cor.12.20; I Peter 2.1). It was frowned upon in rabbinic teaching; several commentators quote the words of Rabbi Asi: 'He who slanders another thereby slanders God.' No one need doubt that it is a very nasty practice. However, James provides a somewhat unusual reason for avoiding it. Those who slander or pass judgement on a fellow Christian, slander and pass judgement on *the law* by their actions. We have already seen that by this term James means Torah, as reinterpreted by Jesus (see the commentary on 2.8). If it is asked how it is possible to *judge* the law, the answer lies in James' characteristic concern with what a person does. *There is only one lawgiver and judge*, he asserts, and that of course, is God. Those who slander and judge other people are thereby breakers of the law, in practice setting it aside as not applicable to them (because they do not obey it). They regard themselves as 'above the law'. But if the sovereign law, defined as love of neighbour (2.8ff.) is indeed the way of life for all Christians, then to set oneself above the law in this way is, effectively, to stand in judgement upon it. Not for the first time in this epistle, living by the way of Christian wisdom involves the radical obedience of faith. The saying of Jesus which James echoes, 'Do not judge and you will not be judged' has, in its Matthean context (Matt. 7.1) a reference to people judging each other (which is forbidden), and the eschatological dimension that refraining from judging others will produce mercy in the judgement (from God). So it is here: God who is judge *is able to save life or destroy it*, but ultimate spiritual destiny is God's prerogative. We are not to pronounce on the fate of another by our attitudes or words.

The danger of wealth
4.13–5.6

This section falls into two separate though related parts, each introduced by the same striking phrase. The first part (4.13–17) is addressed to those engaged in the task of making money, and reminds them that it is futile to plan life other than in accordance with God's will. The second part (5.1–6) is addressed to those who have already made their money, and is a prophetic denunciation of wealth, much harsher in tone than the preceding verses. In both cases the theme of wealth, previously announced at 1.9–11 and to some extent underlying 2.1–7, is a concern, though more so in 5.1–6.

4.13 *Now a word with all who say* is a new form of address; neither the customary 'brothers/friends' nor the 'sinners' of 4.8. It is somewhat abrupt, even argumentative, with the implication that the argument is none too friendly. James is about to rebuke his readers. These people have been making plans for *today or the next day*. They plan to *go off* to another place and spend time there *trading and making money*. Who are they? There is nothing in the immediate context to tell us whether or not they are Christians, though the fact that what they say is cast in the form of vernacular or popular Greek, and rightly put in quotation marks by most modern translations, might suggest that James has overheard such plans being made and has particular people in view. There is also not much point in James addressing them in this way unless they are likely to hear what is said. These considerations suggest that they are Christians, though it is impossible to be sure. What is more certain is that they are traders planning to take advantage of the considerable improvements in travel and communication brought by Roman administration.[1] Whether they are honest or dishonest traders cannot be determined. It is not their business practices as such which James attacks, but their arrogance in assuming that the future lies entirely in their hands, together with the assumption that *making money* is the most important consideration of all. We have seen already that the Jacobean church contained both rich and poor members (see 1.9–11; 2.14–16), though it is obvious enough that the majority of the members were poor, and that the presence of wealthy people in the church was causing some problems. The later Christian writer Clement of Alexandria produced the first systematic discussion in Christian literature of the relationship between faith and wealth, and in his case too, the treatise was made necessary by practical problems in the congregation concerning how the wealthy should be regarded.[2] James does not produce a treatise on the subject, but is obviously concerned that a regard for money does not become dominant in people's lives. The point of the rebuke is not that commerce is somehow unethical in itself, but that the assumptions on which these plans are based are thoroughly secular, both as regards their timing and their content.

4.14 *Yet you* ('you' that is, who are making all these plans with such confidence) *have no idea what tomorrow will bring*. Neither, of course, has anybody else! Awareness of the transitoriness of life is a necessary part of Christian spirituality. The famous words from the Funeral Sentences of the 1662 *Book of Common Prayer*, 'In the midst of life we are in death' say no more than the wise have said in every age. Such sentiments are not intended to encourage morbidity or depression, but to remind human beings of their limitations. One of those limitations is that we do not control with certainty what will happen to us either in the immediate or the longer-term future. The parable of the Rich Fool (Luke 12.16–20) illustrates the point perfectly because there, as here, long-term plans involving worldly wealth are contrasted with that which is unexpected. There are some difficult translation problems in the second part of the verse, though none of them affect the overall sense, which is fairly clear. Life is *no more than a mist*, which comes quickly and then goes with equal suddenness. It has been plausibly suggested that James chose this particular description because the Mediterranean mists would have been especially familiar to the seafaring merchants.[3]

4.15 Now James contrasts what they have said (v.13) with what they *ought to say*, and indeed would say if they were running their lives as people of faith rather than by the world's system of values (4.4). *If it be the Lord's will* is not intended as a pious formula; James offers no encouragement to the tiresome practice of adding 'D.V.'

(an abbreviation of the Latin words for 'God willing') to the announcement of the time of next Sunday's service. What is commended is an attitude of mind. This form of words was used widely in the non-Christian world, where it appears to have functioned in an almost superstitious sense. Its use here is a reminder of the way in which Christians sometimes took over such terms and filled them with new meaning. It is worth noting that Paul frequently expressed this sentiment in relation to his plans to make a first or a return visit to a congregation, or to send or receive a trusted colleague (I Cor. 4.19, 16.7; Rom.1.10; Phil. 2.19,24; Acts 18.21 – though only the first of these is a close verbal parallel to James). The fact that what the traders and merchants *ought* to have said is that, God willing, they would *live to do so and so*, clearly indicates that the planning is not regarded as wrong; what matters is the spirit in which it is done. Those who plan their lives as if they are in complete charge of their own destinies fail to remember that God is sovereign and alone controls the future. Those who remember this and acknowledge it by their attitude of mind are here commended.

4.16   However, these merchants and traders cannot be commended. They *boast and brag*, which probably means that not only do they make the plans which are described in v.13, but they glory in telling everyone else about them. It is bad enough, James suggests, to have such a self-important and God-denying attitude to life; it is even worse that they cannot keep quiet about it. But then, as this epistle has already forcefully pointed out, subduing the tongue is no easy matter!

4.17   *What it comes to* is REB's attempt to give the meaning of the word for 'therefore'. Many other translations leave it out altogether and begin the verse with 'anyone who' or 'everyone who' (RSV/NJB/NIV). The difficulty is that 'therefore' strongly suggests a connection with what has gone before, and it is not very easy to find one here. The statement *anyone who knows the right thing to do and does not do it is a sinner*, is very general and does not seem specially applicable to those who have been castigated for their worldly planning. Even if it was added by an editor or redactor it is difficult to see why it was placed here rather than, for example, after 1.25. It has been widely regarded as a saying which originally circulated independently, even as an otherwise unknown saying of Jesus, but that is pure speculation. It will not quite do to to say that it 'slipped in at this point in the epistle, but without any pretence that it arises out of what has gone before',[4] because the 'therefore' points to the writer's intention that we should see some connection with what has gone before, and REB is correct to indicate this. But what connection are we intended to see? Three possibilities have been canvassed.

The first possibility is that James is drawing on Prov. 3.27–28, which urges the reader not to put off till the morrow the good which should be done today, and in the LXX adds 'you do not know what the morrow will bring forth' (not in the Hebrew text). Since Prov. 3.34 has been quoted at 4.6 this might form a kind of 'afterthought', meaning that omissions will now be counted as sins. This explanation is feeble and does not provide any real connection with the preceding verses. A second possibility is that although on the surface of things James is warning the traders not to forget God in their business plans, he really has the deeper theme of the use of wealth in mind. Their motives for making money ought not to be selfish and worldly ones, but so that they might do the right thing with it, that is, share it with the poor. There is rather more to be said for this explanation since, as we have seen, the importance of keeping money in its proper place *is* present in the writer's mind in the previous verses, and it also offers a link into the next section where that theme emerges with full force. However, such an interpretation, though possible, hardly seems very natural. The third possibility is that the author is saying to the traders: 'I have just told you what you *ought* to do. Now that you know what is the right thing, you are sinners if you fail to do it'. The writer then means that what they ought to do is to take God into account in their thinking and planning. If instead they go ahead with their plans just as they had intended and moreover, boast about it, they need have no doubt that such activity is sinful. There is a difficulty with this explanation as well, notably that the Greek phrase which lies behind the phrase *right thing to do* suggests an action rather than an omission. However, taken all in all, this interpretation is perhaps the least unsatisfactory way of trying to link this verse with what has gone before.[5] But it cannot be denied that this saying has a validity quite independent of the rest of the passage, and expresses an important truth which is not stated in precisely this way elsewhere in the NT (though Rom. 2.17–20 comes close). Given the difficulty of fitting this saying into context, it would be possible to preach a sermon from it which would not violate the old adage, 'a sermon without a context is a pretext.' In such a case, illustrative material might well be drawn from Jesus' saying about the servant who knew his master's wishes, yet failed to carry them out (Luke 12.47).

5.1   *Next a word to you* translates the same phrase with which 4.13 began ('Now a word with all . . .' REB). It is however, used rather differently in this verse. In the earlier passage James proceeds to address a group of people with whose attitudes and plans he is familiar, calling on them to recognize the unsatisfactoriness of their ways and to cease their boasting. Here, what follows is much sharper in tone, there is no expectation of repentance and no description of what they ought to do to put things right. Indeed, in one sense the writer is not directly addressing anyone at all. Those in view are simply people *who are rich*, and the adjective has all the overtones of condemnation it carries at 2.6–7. Here the rich are not members or prospective members of the community, but its enemies. The clue to what James is about comes in the next phrase, where the rich are told to *weep and wail* over their coming fate. This reminds us of the oracles of the OT prophets, who frequently 'addressed' groups and nations who would never have actually heard their words of condemnation. We may think, for example, of Isaiah of Jerusalem's oracle against Babylon, 'Wail, for the day of the Lord is at hand, devastation coming from the Almighty!' (Isa. 13.6), or of Amos's denunciations of the sins of foreign nations as well as those of his own people (Amos 1.3–2.16). The word for *wail* is not found elsewhere in the NT, but comes twenty-one times in the LXX, always in the prophets, where it means 'cry out in lamentation'. The reason why the rich should behave in this way is because of the *miserable fate* which will come their way. This also derives from the tradition of prophetic denunciation (Amos 6.1–7), with the overtone that in the day of judgement God himself will vindicate the poor (Ps. 12.5). This is why James 'addresses' the rich in such a manner; not because they are going to read what he writes, but for the warning and encouragement of the community as a whole. Warning, because if any of the rich or potentially rich Christians (such as the merchants and traders previously addressed) are tempted to believe that their riches are in themselves of any benefit, they need to be reminded that wealth is a source of trouble and difficulty rather than blessing. Encouragement, because rich people have been the oppressors of the community and no doubt in the process seemed to have all the power and authority on their side. By reminding his fellow Christians of the coming judgement on the rich, the author encourages them to look beyond any immediate troubles they may be experiencing to the time when they will be vindicated by God. From this starting-point, James spells out in more detail both his charges against the rich and their expected fate. In so doing he draws not only on the prophetic tradition of the OT, but also on the teaching of Jesus.

5.2–3 *Your riches have rotted away* strikes us as slightly odd in view of what has gone before. If the writer is looking towards the final judgement on the rich we would expect him to say, 'your riches will rot away'. In fact he uses what we would call the past tense three times. Not only have the riches already rotted, but their *fine clothes are moth-eaten* and their *silver and gold have corroded*. The usual explanation is that James is using the 'prophetic perfect'.[6] This form is often found, especially in Second Isaiah, to describe coming events as though they had already happened (Isa. 40.2; 44.23; 46.1 etc.). It imparts extra vividness to the writing and also says something about the certainty of the coming events. However, it is striking that the writer goes on to say that the *corrosion* of the gold and silver *will be evidence against* the rich. It seems that he is charging them with having preferred to let moths and rust devour their wealth, rather than using it to help the needy.[7] This thought certainly appears in the Jewish Wisdom literature: 'Be ready to lose money for a brother or a friend rather than leave it to rust away under a stone. Dispose of your treasure as commanded by the Most High; that will benefit you more than gold' (Ecclus. 29.10–11). If so, then the teaching of Jesus about wealth is here used in a way closer to its Lukan context than its Matthean (Luke 12.33 rather than Matt. 6.19). In Matthew's sermon Jesus urges his hearers not to accumulate treasure on earth, because such treasure is perishable: moth and rust destroy it and (this last is not in James), thieves break in and steal. In contrast, people should store up treasure in heaven, because such treasure will be imperishable. In Luke's text the reference to the provision of treasure in heaven remains, but the command is added to sell possessions and give to charity in the present. James however has nothing about treasure in heaven, and the perishability is somewhat subsidiary to the weeping and wailing and the coming judgement. The implication is that the treasures on earth have indeed perished, but it is because they have not been used properly. This is not inconsistent with the view that the writer may be using the 'prophetic perfect', because in the coming judgement the treasure will perish in reality, reflecting the fact that its value is already illusory.

The stark image that the corrosion will itself *consume your flesh like fire* is again a pointer forward to judgement, as is the assertion that the rich have *piled up wealth in an age that is near its close*. The phrase might be rendered more literally: 'You have hoarded wealth in the last days.' James might well be thinking that the end of the world was shortly to arrive, which appears to be the meaning in 5.8. Or he could be expressing the view that following the death and resurrection of Jesus the last days have in some sense already arrived. Some commentators have discerned an ironic tone in this phrase: the rich have piled up wealth with an eye to the future, whereas the only future which does await them is misery and judgement. They would have done much better to have accumulated the kind of treasure which is imperishable – though James does not spell that out.

In one sense, these verses read oddly to modern ears, at least in Western societies where wealth is thought of in terms of land, shares and bank accounts. James is simply using contemporary Middle Eastern indications of wealth; fine clothes which could be inherited but could also be attacked by moths, grain which represented plenty with which to trade but could rot, as well as the more enduring silver and gold which remain to this day as signs of a person's wealth.

5.4   The idea that James' main concern is that riches have not been used properly receives some support from his next charge. The rich, we now learn, are landowners. Even though earning a living from the land is not always an easy matter, the ownership of land, especially on a large scale, is one of the most secure of all forms of wealth. The supply of land is fixed and it is needed for many purposes. There is evidence that in the world of James' day, large landowners exerted considerable power over the lives of others, not least through absenteeism and through their influence on the judicial processes.[8] Here, it is specific injustice against their employees which is under discussion. This took two forms, the first of which was that they *never paid* the wages of those who worked for them. Such a failure was specifically forbidden by the Law of Moses (Lev. 19.13) and in the prophetic literature those who broke this regulation are condemned by God alongside adulterers and perjurers (Mal. 3.5). Interestingly, it is the withheld wages themselves which are crying aloud against these unjust rich, rather in the way in which the blood of the murdered Abel was said to cry out to God from the ground (Gen. 4.10). Indeed, that image may well be in the writer's mind because he views all this oppression as murderous (v.6). The accusation reaches a climax with *the outcry of the reapers has reached the ears of the Lord of Hosts.* Here we have a solemn title for God, emphasizing power and majesty, coupled with the deplorable situation of the poorest and neediest in society. Those who have been defrauded of their wages, and presumably thereby left literally destitute, can be assured that their anguished cries are not uttered into the empty air, but into the ears of Almighty God. There could hardly be a stronger statement of God's concern for social justice or a clearer indication that the God who is interested only in 'spiritual' things is not the God of James (nor, we may add, of Jesus). Or perhaps we may prefer to say, quite properly, that social justice *is* a spiritual matter.

5.5   James repeats, though in different words, the thought which has already found expression in v.3, now even more strongly. The wealthy agriculturalists have not only piled up wealth for themselves in a passive sense, and by failing to use it properly have deprived the poor and needy of what they should have received; they have actively lived off their land in *wanton luxury*, for which their gluttony is cited as proof. However, without realizing it, they have really been fattening themselves up for the day of their *slaughter.* This is the way REB understands the phrase, and it is preferable to seeing it as a metaphor derived from the unrestrained feasting of victors after a battle.[9] The OT has a number of gory pictures in which the day of God's judgement on his enemies is the day of slaughter (e.g. Isa. 30.25; 34.5–8; Jer. 50.26–27) even though the actual phrase is never used. There is irony in what the rich have been doing, just as there was at the end of v.3. The end which is in store for the rich reminds some commentators of the story of Dives and Lazarus (Luke 16.19–31, esp. v.25), but the parallels are not really very close despite the hint here in James of the reversal of fortunes. A closer parallel, in thought though not in wording, is with the insistence of Jesus that certain kinds of people have had their reward already. In Matthew it is applied to those who engage in charitable works or fasting ostentatiously and for the wrong motives (Matt. 6.2,16). Here too, it appears, the rich have had their reward. Since all they cared about was the pleasure of accumulating wealth in order to spend it on themselves, they have another sort of fate awaiting them, which cannot be described as a reward in any except the most ironic sense.

5.6   The final charge against the rich is damning; to *condemn and murder the innocent one* takes us back in the first instance to v.4 where defrauding the poor of their rights is in mind. By reducing people to penury, perhaps to actual starvation, they have effectively condemned and murdered people whose only crime was to be less powerful and less influential than themselves. However, this phrase also seems to have legal overtones. One of the marks of a just and civilized society is that its legal system is fair and honest, providing justice regardless of the social or financial status of those involved. We have already seen James' concern about this in the context of a 'church court' in 2.1–13. If, as seems probable, the rich and power-ful of the day were able to use their influence to manipulate justice so that the poor were oppressed, that could certainly be regarded as a kind of judicial murder. It is possible that the practice which is in mind is of rich people getting poor people into their clutches through debt, and then using the provisions of the law on debt to reduce them to abject poverty. We cannot be certain about this, but whatever the precise background it is clear that the wealthy were engaging in some quite unjust and wholly unacceptable practices, which James here condemns in the strongest possible terms. There is no need to look for a reference to Jesus in the phrase *the innocent one*, though it is used in that way at Acts 3.14, 7.52 and 22.14. There is no real evidence to suggest that the rich condemned and killed Jesus, even allowing for the involvement of the rich Sadducees in the process which led to the crucifixion. The term here stands as a symbol of all those who are righteous and innocent, because their trust is in God alone. The righteous or innocent one, it is said, *offers no resistance*. This is because, of course, none is possible. The rich and powerful hold all the cards in their hands, in worldly terms. It is thus even more important to emphasize, as James does, that in the final analysis, on judgement day itself, they will not do so. Yet there is a sense in which the author is not complaining about the fact that no resistance is offered. The fact that the innocent cannot and do not resist, shows up the evil of the oppression for what it really is. Those being oppressed are no threat to anyone – though they are a threat to those who want all the wealth and power for themselves. Indeed, there is no indication in what James writes in this passage that the destruction of the rich and the exaltation of the poor are in anyone's hands except God's.[10] If our interpretation of 4.1–4 is correct, then we meet the same attitude here too: God's kingdom and righteousness cannot be brought in by force of any kind, but God will himself bring it in, for he has promised it to the poor and downtrodden (2.5).

There is an inevitable question about what this passage means for contemporary Christians, especially in prosperous countries. It is probably true that few people ever perceive themselves as 'rich', but in comparison with a large proportion of the world's population many of us are exactly that. James has some devastating things to say about the rich, their greed, their hoarding, their dishonesty and their oppressiveness. It is too easy to dismiss such charges as applicable only to other people, especially if we do not feel ourselves personally culpable in this regard. Yet the dilemma of rich Christians in a world of poverty is a real one. To the extent that we are caught up in the mechanisms of highly developed consumer-oriented societies we are all compromised sinners, and that needs to be recognized. Appropriate responses to James' charges will be a matter of individual conscience, but at the very least ought to involve a concern for fair world trade and political liberty. If that involves rich Christians in paying higher prices for some of the goods they consume, as well as higher taxes in order to help inter-governmental aid to become realistic, it is a fair price to pay. In the light of James' words, charity is not enough.

Patience and prayer
5.7–20

This final segment of the epistle, as it appears in the structure adopted by REB, falls into four sections. The first of these (vv. 7–11) is better linked with 4.13–5.6, since its theme of patience under trial really flows out of the preceding reflections on the oppressive behaviour of the wealthy. The remaining sections deal with truthful speaking (v.12), healing and prayer (vv.13–18) and pastoral care (vv.19–20). It is not easy to find an overall title for these, other than a very general one such as 'community concerns'. Here, more than anywhere else in the epistle we can see the hand of the editor, who possessed material too important to be left out, but which could not be logically placed anywhere else. In some cases it is possible to discern thematic relationships with what has gone before, but there is no logical sequence of thought. For example, the teaching on oaths at v.12 can be viewed as one aspect of Christian speaking, but it could not easily have been placed with the material of 3.1–12 because of its particular emphasis. In this concluding segment, with the exception of the relationship of vv.7–11 to what has gone before, we should not look for any very close connections between the topics.

5.7 The exhortation to be *patient, my friends, until the Lord comes*, reminds us that early in the epistle, James stated the need to endure trials and testings and to stand up to them (1.2–4, 12). Many of the significant trials which the epistle has in view come from the oppressive actions of the rich (2.6; 5.1–6). Following the 'address' to the rich, in which their sure fate is described, James now turns again to the members of the faithful community and, in the face of what some of them are having to endure, counsels patience. If judgement is coming to the wealthy oppressors (which it is), then in the meantime the proper attitude of the oppressed is to *be patient*. Advice to adopt a passive attitude might seem strange coming from this author, who so frequently insists on the need for actions, but he has already indicated that God's cause is not served by human anger (1.20) and God's rule cannot be brought in by forceful human behaviour (4.1–4). Nevertheless, this waiting is not envisaged entirely passively. It is to be an expectant and hopeful waiting, because the action will come from God. The term for the Lord's coming is *parousia*, which normally in the NT is a term for the coming of Christ (e.g. Matt. 24.3,37,39; I Cor. 15.23; I Thess. 2.19, 3.13; I John. 2.28). Some have hesitated to take it in that sense here on the grounds that the 'Lord' of v.4 is obviously God and the overall context is judgement. However, there is no good reason to see this as anything other than a reference to the coming of Christ. It is standard NT teaching that the 'second coming' will be a time of judgement, involving not only vindication for the righteous, but punishment for evildoers, not least for those who afflict the righteous (II Thess. 1.4–10). To illustrate the need for patience, the author adduces the example of the *farmer* who longs for the *precious crop* which is the result of all his previous hard work in sowing and tending but who, when he has done everything he can, must *wait in patience until the early and late rains have fallen*. This illustration has all the marks of being a picture which is familiar to the readers of the epistle, one of several which James draws from peasant life.[1] It makes a contrast with the rich agriculturalists and large landowners of vv. 1–6; this farmer is obviously what we would call a smallholder who works his own land and is understandably anxious to see the results of the labours on which his welfare, and that of his family depends. Such a person might have figured amongst the victims of larger and more rapacious landowners. The reference to the timing of the rains is often cited, with good reason, as an indication that the epistle has a Syro-Palestinian provenance, since the phenomenon, necessary for proper growth, is confined to that part of the Mediterranean. However that may be, the point of the illustration is the patient waiting.

5.8 The point is reinforced; like the farmer, Christians must be *patient*, and to this is now added the advice to be *stout-hearted*. Literally this reads 'establish your hearts' and is an exhortation to remain firm and faithful in the time of trial. Indeed, the end is in sight because *the coming of the Lord is near*. As in the previous verse, this is a reference to the coming of Christ in glory and in judgement; but what does James mean by *near*? The logic of his argument must mean that he expects the return of Christ to take place in the near future; otherwise the counselling of patience loses much of its point.

Expectation of the imminent return of Christ is characteristic of the earlier documents of the NT rather than the later ones. Indeed, what is sometimes termed the 'delay of the parousia' was one of the problems with which Christians had to come to terms, especially when, contrary to their expectations, some of their number died before the Lord returned.[2] This is a highly complex issue, concerning which there is no overall agreement amongst scholars. No doubt its importance in shaping the theologies of the NT has sometimes been exaggerated, but it was a real problem and in the writings of Paul in particular we can trace how it was dealt with.[3] In large part the difficulty was resolved by using parousia language to stress the importance of being *ready* for the Lord's return, whenever that might be, rather than taking it to refer to an event which could certainly be expected within a short period of time. There is no sense in James that such a problem exists. The writer simply refers to the return of the Lord as *near*, and the context is not readiness but imminent expectation preceded by patient waiting. From our present perspective, we realize that James was mistaken in this expectation and, as J. B. Adamson says, 'we must adapt ourselves, and his teaching, to the delay.'[4] In terms of our understanding of the parousia itself, this is not too difficult. We can follow the lead of those who in the first Christian century interpreted it to mean that each and every generation has to live in readiness, as if it might be the last (Matt. 25.1–13). But if we no longer expect, as James did, that Christ will return in the near future to set things right, what becomes of his teaching on the need for patient waiting until that happens? To counsel the oppressed and downtrodden to wait patiently for a very short time, at the end of which there will be justice for them, is a rather different matter from advocating long-term patience in the face of manifest injustice. We cannot, of course, know what James would have said had he lived to know that his time-scale was mistaken. We must wrestle with what he did say, remembering his own frequent insistence that genuine faith is radical obedience and loving action.

5.9   The Christian community is under pressure, and a period of waiting is involved. It is only human nature (even redeemed human nature), to look for someone who can be blamed for the difficulties which are being experienced. It would be natural to lay blame at the door of the rich persecutors (vv.1–6) and James does not suggest that would be wrong. However, for members of the community to blame their troubles *on one another* would be a quite different matter, and would cause unnecessary friction which would add to their difficulties. Any community facing problems needs its members to be mutually supportive. That is no more than simple commonsense, though sometimes hard to achieve. However, there is more involved than simple commonsense. We have already seen that when Christians speak ill of each other, or give way to anger, God's purposes are not served (1.19–20). It is also true that engaging in personal rivalries and jealousies leads to actual strife (3.14–16), and that those who speak ill of one another have stopped living by the Christian law of love (4.11–12). If then, the Christian community is to retain the integrity which it should rightly possess in order to be worthy of being called Christian, its members must avoid blaming one another for their common plight. To do otherwise would be to give in to those trials and tests which should be endured steadfastly and thus lead to perfection (1.4). As at 4.12, there is only one *Judge* and (in another reference to the early expectation of the parousia) he stands *at the door*. To live in the interim without blaming each other is a practical example of what it means to be patient, and it is to this topic that James now returns directly.

5.10–11a   For a general illustration of patience in the face of suffering, the writer refers to *the prophets who spoke in the name of the Lord*. He does not as yet specify any particular prophets, and evidently intended his readers to supply their own examples from their knowledge of the OT scriptures and perhaps from stories of brave people from the inter-testamental period. We need not suppose that he has those we think of as 'the prophets' exclusively in mind; the instruction would include all those whose stand for true faith in the midst of persecution constituted a witness to God. Some of the heroes and heroines of the Maccabean period would supply notable instances of people who *stood firm*, even to the point of martyrdom, and in places their stories are told in an evidently hagiographical manner (e.g. II Macc. 7). For the examples of *patience* the readers might have looked to the way in which some of the canonical prophets had to continue to deliver their messages from God patiently and persistently, despite the unwillingness of God's people to listen to them (Isa. 6.9–13; Jer.20.8; Ezek. 2.4–11). Those who thus lived faithfully through difficult times are counted *happy*. James is not pronouncing a blessing upon them, but rather alluding to the tradition with which both he and his readers are familiar, that they are by common consent so regarded; their stories are part of the true story of faith down the ages. Blessedness springs from faithfulness, as it does in Matt. 5.10.

5.11b   The writer moves from the general illustration to the specific example of *Job*. The AV translation, which refers to 'the patience of Job' has bequeathed a phrase to the English language, indicating patience which is exceptional and outstanding. Unfortunately, this is not quite the impression which we receive from reading the Book of Job itself. Modern translations properly refer, as does REB, to the way in which *Job stood firm*, which somewhat lessens the difficulty. Job hardly exhibited what we would regard as patience, especially with those who in his judgement argued foolishly (e.g. Job 13.1–5); nor do his complaints to God about his plight suggest a man of great patience (e.g. Job 2; 13.3). Commentators often suggest that James is drawing on widely-known traditions about Job not in our canonical book of that name, but which find expression in a document known as the *Testament of Job*.[5] In this apocryphal book most of the complaining is done by Job's wife (see Job 2.9–10) whilst he becomes a much more positive figure. It is not necessary to suppose that James had read this; the narratives which make it up were no doubt in common circulation long before they were written down. If an attempt is to be made to find ways in which the Book of Job itself points to Job's steadfastness under trial, we might consider Job. 1.21; 19.25–27. However, it may be better not to look for specific texts in this connection, but to consider the thrust of the Book of Job as a whole. This is notoriously difficult, but at least this much may be said: when in ch. 31 Job sets out the record of his good deeds, he is staking his claim to be regarded as a blameless and upright man, just as he is described in Job 1.1–5, which needs to be taken seriously.[6] The whole point of Job's increasing distress and bewilderment at his sufferings is that he has done nothing to deserve them, and he knows that he has not. To the end he refuses to give in to the seductive voices of his friends who insist, particularly in the third cycle of speeches, that he must be a great sinner or else he would not be suffering so much (Job 22.3–30). Indeed, they eventually give up their attempts precisely because he 'continued to think himself righteous' (Job 32.1). It is extremely difficult for a modern Christian reader not to read Job through Christian (even Lutheran Christian) spectacles; to realize in fact, that it was perfectly appropriate for Job to think of himself as righteous. As John Gibson expresses it: 'his essential goodness and sincerity, his integrity if you like, is, although impugned by his friends, never doubted by himself nor, more importantly, overturned by God. A coming to terms with "grace" in the Pauline sense and a giving up of belief in the effectiveness of good works, are not among the lessons he has to learn.[7] This is surely what James, of all people, must mean when he refers to the way Job stood firm, and adds *you have seen how the Lord treated him in the end* – a reference to the restoration of all that Job had before his troubles began, and more (Job 42.10b-17). Of course, James is not suggesting to his readers that they should emulate Job in his self-understanding, only that by clinging to the end to the one thing he was sure of, he became an outstanding example of an endurance under trial which does not compromise integrity. The close of Job's story shows how *the Lord is merciful and compassionate*; the end of the story of a suffering yet patient community will show the same thing, though through vindication and spiritual blessings rather than material riches.

5.12 This verse constitutes a topic in itself. As we have noted, it has to do with Christian speaking, so it is not an entirely new subject, but would not have fitted well into the previous discussion. The phrase *above all* would seem to indicate that the subject about to be discussed is the most important with which the writer has yet dealt. Since he has previously referred to murder, adultery, and false faith amongst other things, this seems implausible. Some commentators take it as an indication of a new topic, but the repetition of *my friends* ('brothers') would signal that on its own. Others think it is a sign that the epistle is now drawing to a close. We simply cannot be certain what it means; to take it as some kind of indication that what follows is important and demands respect, is about as near as we can get.

The command, *do not use oaths* is not a reference to what we sometimes call 'bad language' nor, of course, to the more technical sense of the oath one may be called upon to take in a court of law, although some application to both those situations may perhaps be derived from what is said here. The taking of oaths, or 'swearing' as it is otherwise called, particularly applied to someone who 'swore' not to perform a particular action, even though that action was not regarded as intrinsically bad, as in 'I swear that I will not eat meat for a month.' Something of this sense is retained in the slightly archaic English word 'forswear', which describes an act of rejecting, renouncing or denying in a solemn manner. Oaths and vows were of considerable interest to rabbinic Judaism, which legislated extensively in regard to them.[8] It would seem that by NT times, certainly in popular usage, such oaths were often reinforced by appeal to some divine symbol in order to impress people with the truthfulness of what was being said: 'I swear by heaven that I will not eat meat for a month.' According to Matthew's Gospel, Jesus responded to this common practice with some direct words (Matt. 5.33–37), and here we find James reiterating his teaching. The simplest way to demonstrate the relationship between the two texts is to follow the admirable example of C. L. Mitton[9] and reproduce the teaching of Jesus as Matthew records it, printing in italics the words which are also in James:[10]

> You are *not to use oaths* at all – *whether 'by heaven'*, for it is God's throne, *or 'by earth'*, for it is his footstool, nor by Jerusalem, for it is the city of the great King, nor by your own head, because you cannot turn one hair of it white or black. *Plain "Yes" or "No" is all you need to say*; anything beyond that comes from the evil one.

It is extremely likely that the nucleus of this teaching of Jesus, shorn of the illustrations which arose from Palestinian Jewish practice , ran: 'You are not to use oaths at all. Plain "Yes" or "No" is all you need to say; anything beyond that comes from the evil one.'[11] The early Christian writer Justin Martyr quotes it in almost exactly this form, and describes it as a 'command not to swear at all, but always to speak the truth'.[12] It is not possible to determine whether Justin omits the illustrative material because it was of no interest to him or because he was in touch with an independent oral source, but it demonstrates something of the impact which the teaching had on the early Christian communities. Here in James we find the original saying, consisting of three elements: (i) do not swear/use oaths, (ii) Yes and No is all you need, (iii) anything more comes from the evil one. In James' version, the third part of this appears slightly differently as: *for fear you draw down judgement on yourselves*, but this is not a problem. It was axiomatic that every human thought or action which came from the evil one would be condemned by God in the final judgement.[13] To this nucleus James adds two of the specific illustrations also in Matthew ('by heaven' and 'by earth') but does not include Matthew's reasons. In place of the material about Jerusalem and changing the colour of one's hair, James offers an all-embracing *or by anything else*, as if to make it plain that the examples are only examples and one ought not to try and get round them by casuistically arguing that one has sworn by something which is not prohibited! As we have seen, this epistle is almost certainly earlier than Matthew's Gospel, and so James cannot be quoting from it. What we have here is an earlier form of the teaching of Jesus, and an independent witness to it. The sayings circulated in the various Christian communities, and were doubtless used for the purposes of teaching new converts, before being incorporated in the writings as we now have them. This version seems to be an intermediate one between the 'nucleus' and the final form we have in Matthew. Its emphasis on the judgement which will result from breaking the command fits well with James' concern about how other sins also lead to judgement (2.12–13; 4.8,12; 5.3–5,9).

There is no doubting the frequency with which this epistle alludes to the teaching of Jesus (see the Introduction: 'James and Jesus'; some commentators have argued for rather more such allusions than we have accepted), but this is by far the clearest. In itself this highlights the importance of this particular teaching to the first Christians. It was not regarded as being of secondary concern, but as a distinctive mark of discipleship. The reason for this is not far to seek, and it aids our understanding of what this text means for us today. The command not to use oaths is not so much about the words spoken, at least not in themselves. It is about what they reveal concerning the speaker's character. Related to this specific command is the insight of Matt. 12.34: 'How can your words be good when you yourselves are evil? It is from the fullness of the heart that the mouth speaks.' Those who constantly supplement their statements with, 'I swear to you' and 'on God's honour', or even the children's oath, 'cross my heart and hope to die', only indicate one thing: they do not otherwise expect to be believed. The teaching of Jesus and James envisages Christians whose characters are such that their speech is always 'true' and this can be recognized by others. Those who practise such radical truthfulness have no need to use oaths, because their integrity will be such that their simple word can be accepted.

Of course, James is not entering into a debate on how Christians conduct themselves with regard to the common decencies of everyday life. If the answer to the question, 'Do you like my new dress/tie?' is 'No', there are ways of returning that answer which combine truth with tact. The important question is whether someone's word can be trusted. James demands that Christians be the sort of people whose word *can* be trusted, not because they tell you so and reinforce the telling with solemn oaths, but because they are people whose truthfulness comes from hearts which are in tune with God. If we could imagine a Christian community which obeyed this command, and whose members could totally rely on each other's truthfulness, we could imagine a world transformed.

5.13   The section which begins here deals with healing and prayer. *Is anyone among you in trouble?* The troubles envisaged would seem to exclude illness, which is dealt with separately. We have seen various kinds of troubles alluded to in the epistle and some of them may be intended here, even though previous passages dealing with persecution, for example, have not especially mentioned prayer in that context (1.2–4; 2.6). Here perhaps, more personal troubles are in mind. If some of the unchristian behaviour described earlier in the epistle, in relation to discrimination (2.1–4), lack of love in action (2.14–16), wrong attitudes (3.14–16), wrong ambitions and actions (4.1–4), slander and gossip (4.11–12) and people blaming one another for the community's problems (5.9) are to be related to real-life situations familiar to the readers, then the more sensitive and spiritually aware members of the community would certainly be greatly troubled by such behaviour, especially if they had been the victims of it. Perhaps only those engaged in the pastoral work of the church know how much of their time is often spent in helping others through the suffering the Lord's people sometimes inflict on one another by unworthy behaviour and attitudes. Or James might be referring to such troubles as come the way of every human being, and from which Christians are certainly not exempt. But whatever the cause, when people are suffering or in trouble, they are to *pray*. Nothing is said about the content of such prayers, nor about their expected effect. Prayer of this kind should try not to tell God what the answer is, but be content to lay the situation which is causing the distress before God. Sometimes, when troubles appear overwhelming, it is not easy to find the words for prayer, and such a simple offering of need to God is all that can be done; it is sufficient. Conversely, anyone who is *in good heart* should *sing praises* (literally, 'psalms'). It is an observable fact of human life that people who make no real profession of religious faith often do turn to God in prayer when they are in trouble, but that people who should know they have much to be thankful for often forget to express their gratitude to God in an appropriate way! James therefore reminds them of the rightness of voicing such gratitude. We may recall the experience of the Quaker George Fox, who, in religious despair sought counsel from an 'ancient priest' in Warwickshire in 1645. He was told to 'take tobacco and sing psalms'. Fox commented: 'Tobacco was a thing I did not love, and psalms I was not in a state to sing.' There is some practical wisdom in James's distinction between praying and singing, even if the two are in many respects closely related.

5.14 Those who are troubled or in good heart are offered appropriate responses to their respective conditions, and the text suggests that both the prayer and the singing may be undertaken privately. If someone is *ill* however, it is clearly envisaged that the Christian community has a role to play. The sick person should *send for the elders of the church*. It may be noted in passing, that those with pastoral responsibility in the church are not credited with supernatural powers by which they should know that someone is ill without having been told; the sick person, who is presumably too ill to attend the community gathering, has a responsibility to invite them to come to the home. The *elders* were probably a specific office in the early church, though as in the case of teachers (see the commentary on 3.1) we cannot be quite sure what their office entailed, nor how it might be distinguished from other offices. The establishment of the office of Christian elders is sometimes held to have been based on that of Jewish elders in the synagogues, but this is far from certain.[14] The main NT references come in the Pastoral Epistles and especially Acts (11.30; 14.23; 15.2; 16.4; 20.17 and 21.18). R.P. Martin points to the significance of that last reference, since it shows a scene where elders 'gather round James, who is the head of a collegium.'[15] From several of these passages it is clear that their responsibilities included the pastoral care of others. In translating this into contemporary terms we should think of those who are appointed to undertake such care within the Christian community, regardless of the title by which they are known. When the *elders* reach the sick person, they have two things to do to: they must *pray* over the one who is sick, and *anoint him with oil in the name of the Lord*. The prayer (as the next verse makes quite clear) is for the healing of the one who is ill. It is quite important that, as James pictures it, the *elders* perform their tasks as a group, and also as a matter of course through their pastoral ministry. Paul knows of those to whom the Spirit has given 'gifts of healing' (I Cor. 12.9), but such individual gifts are not in mind here. This practice is a normal part of congregational life in a church which appears to know nothing whatever of the 'charismatic gifts' discussed in the Pauline correspondence. Nor, for that matter, is there any reference to the laying on of hands (though Mark 16.18 might be considered a sufficient authority for that practice).

To *pray* with and for the sick is a natural enough practice within the community of faith; but what is the significance of the anointing with oil? The word James uses for *anoint* occurs eight times in the NT, but only one of those (Mark 6.13) is in connection with healing the sick. The use of oil for medicinal purposes is a procedure widely attested in the ancient world, and it has been suggested that this is its meaning here, thus forming a contemporary illustration of the medical methods of healing which James commends along with the prayer.[16] This is an attractive interpretation, because it allows us to stress the undoubted truth that both medical techniques and prayer are part of what Christians understand by healing. However, it has to be questioned whether this is what the writer intends. If the anointing was for standard medicinal purposes, why is its administration confined to the group of elders? Furthermore, does not the fact that the anointing is to be done *in the name of the Lord* point to its essential character as a religious act? If so, the OT tradition that oil stands as a symbol of gladness and plenty, and that anointing with oil in times of special need symbolizes God's favour and presence, may lie behind what is commended (Isa.61.3; Pss.23.5; 45.7; 133.2; Prov.27.9). To anoint in the Lord's name evidently involves calling on the Lord for healing whilst doing so.

5.15   Anointing is not therefore a magical technique which will automatically produce the desired result, but an accompaniment to the prayer. It is the *prayer offered in faith* which will *heal the sick*. The word translated *heal* has the wider meaning of 'save', and James has already used it three times with that meaning (1.21; 2.14; 4.12). Some translations prefer it here as well (AV; RV; RSV; JB; NJB), but it is unlikely that it refers to final salvation on the last day. REB chooses the more probable meaning of healing from physical illness in this life and restoration to health by *the Lord*. There is a progression of thought in these verses. The anointing does not by itself accomplish the healing; there must be prayer offered in *faith*. If we refer back to 1.5–8 we can see what kind of prayer the writer envisages; it must be prayer which does not doubt and is not double-minded. It is certainly the faith of the elders of the church, rather than the sick person, which must lie behind such prayer. Yet neither does the prayer in itself accomplish the healing; that is the Lord's work in response to the fervent request which has been offered. REB slightly obscures the nature of the Lord's action: James says 'the Lord will raise him up', using the verb 'to raise' which is found elsewhere in the NT to describe the new strength which comes to those who have received physical healing (Matt. 9.6; Acts 3.7).

What James says certainly poses some problems for the contemporary church, because his statement that faithful prayer will result in healing is unqualified. This was not the experience of Paul (II Cor. 12.8–9) nor of others in the early church (II Tim. 4.20), and it is not our experience either. Pretending that it *ought* to be our experience is a cruel deception, for when such prayer does not 'work', an explanation has to be sought. All too frequently the one offered is that the sick person does not have sufficient faith (despite, as we have seen, the 'faith' in this passage being that of the elders and not the sick person). In addressing a situation in which physical healing is always given, James speaks outside the context which we know. For this and other reasons, those who work in the Christian healing ministry often prefer to speak of a 'wholeness' which is God's gift to the sufferer, whether or not physical healing takes place. This is a very large subject which cannot be treated in any depth here,[17] but support for this approach can still be found in the verb 'save' in this verse. Granted, as we must, that the writer seems to view it in terms of physical healing, that is not the only meaning it can carry. Nor do we have to make a straight choice between physical healing now and salvation on the last day. Sometimes the word is used in the sense of 'rescue' or 'deliverance' from some peril, as when the disciples and Peter specifically, thought themselves in danger of sinking (Matt. 8.25; 14.30). It can also refer to being delivered from the corruption of the world around (Acts 2.40), and in Luke's account of how Zaccheus came to his senses Jesus declares that the purpose of his coming is to 'save' people from lostness (Luke 19.10). Restoration to wholeness and to a place of safety is not absent from this word, even if James has a somewhat narrower meaning in view.

Support for thinking in these wider terms is found in what comes next: *if he has committed sins they will be forgiven*. We certainly need to notice the *if*, which is not accidental. The relationship between sin and suffering has teased and puzzled the human mind down the centuries, and is a major question in the Book of Job, on which James has already drawn (v.11). The gospels record healings performed by Jesus in which there is no connection between the illness and sin, but others in which there clearly is such a relationship (Mark 2.1–12;

Matt. 9.2–8). Any attempt to automatically ascribe affliction to sin is ruled out by Jesus in the Fourth Gospel (John 9.1–3). The idea that physical illness may on occasion have its origins in sin and subsequent guilt can hardly be denied. If this should be so in any particular case, then the healing does indeed need to concern itself with a wholeness which includes the forgiveness of sins. Again, it is clear from the text that such forgiveness is from the Lord, though those who minister pastorally as elders doubtless have the task of declaring such forgiveness to the sick person.

5.16 What is good and right in the case of a member of the community undergoing the affliction of illness, is also good and right for the community as a whole; consideration of the individual case leads the writer into a more general instruction. *Confess your sins to one another* presupposes a mutual trust, such as is often found in the early days of a religious movement. When, in the formative years of the Methodist revival, John Wesley followed a Moravian custom with which he was familiar, and placed certain of his followers in 'Bands' or, even more exclusively, 'select societies', mutual confession was expected of those who participated. Members were routinely asked, 'What sins have you committed since our last meeting?' Some older Methodist churches still possess a 'Band Room' which has nothing to do with church orchestras, but everything to do with meeting together to urge one another on to Christian perfection. Such practices seem almost impossible to sustain once the initial fervour of the revival has cooled down, and in the case of the Methodist Class Meetings and Bands there is evidence that, despite the mythology which is sometimes attached to them, they did not function for very long in the way originally intended.[18] The problems with such practices are obvious and it would be naive to ignore them. Nevertheless, the ideal which James commends ought not to be passed over lightly. Such mutual confession stands in direct contrast to the mutual grumbling of v.9, and the openness which it suggests argues for far more committed relationships within the Body of Christ than we customarily experience, at least in Western societies. At the very least James is commending admission of the sins Christians have committed against one another (Matt. 5.23–24), though he intends to go beyond that. Only when such openness is a reality can the command to *pray for one another* be properly fulfilled, because only then are the true needs of others known to the interceder. The purpose of such mutual confession and prayer is summed up by *that you may be healed*, which refers to the spiritual health of the community as a whole rather than specific individuals within it. None should doubt that such a result is possible, because the prayer of a *good* person is *very powerful and effective*. We do not need to look for any specific *good* person here; the writer means that those who are living the Christian life as it should be lived, by the sovereign law (2.8) make powerful and effective prayers. It is not that God is unwilling to listen to anybody else, but that the *good*, being friends of God rather than friends of the world, pray from right motives and for what is in tune with God's will (4.3–4), and their prayer can be answered accordingly.

5.17–18 For his fourth and final example from the OT, James chooses *Elijah*. The reason for the choice lies in the assertion that Elijah was *a man just like us*, which tells us that he shared in normal human limitations. One of the dangers of using biblical examples to illustrate a point, is that hearers might say: 'That is all very well; but Elijah was somebody special, one of God's great prophets. You would expect *his* prayers to be effective, but we cannot expect the same result from our prayers.' James counters any temptation to think in this way with his statement that the readers and Elijah share a common human nature. If his prayers could be powerful, so can ours be. The specific incident in Elijah's colourful career to which the writer alludes is recorded in I Kings 17.1–18.45, culminating in the contest with the prophets of Baal on Mount Carmel. The narrative does not explicitly record that Elijah prayed for the drought to begin, as James suggests, though he does tell King Ahab, 'there will be neither dew nor rain these coming years unless I give the word.' (I Kings 17.1). There is a strong suggestion that it was the prayer of Elijah which brought it to an end (I Kings 18.42–45), though again, this is not explicitly stated. It may be that James is drawing on traditional interpretations of Elijah's actions which would have been familiar to his readers. One such is found in Ecclus. 48.3 which, in the course of recounting his deeds says: 'By the word of the Lord he shut up the sky.' It is something of a puzzle why James does not choose other instances of Elijah's praying which would have served his purpose as well, or better (such as the prayer on behalf of the widow's son, I Kings 18.20–22, or the prayer on Mount Carmel, I Kings 18.36–7). The suggestion that the dry and dead earth of the drought mirrors how the sick Christian might feel,[19] seems somewhat far-fetched. However, the final reference to the consequence of

the drought's ending, *the land bore crops once more*, is nowhere
stated in the Kings narrative (though, of course, it is a logical enough
consequence!) It might be just a piece of illustrative embroidery, but
more likely it is intended as a reminder that when the members of
the Christian community pray for one another in the way James has
recommended, the result is a fruitful and healthy community life.

5.19–20 As the epistle nears its close, we meet the characteristic
address *my friends* for the last time. The resemblance to I John 5.21
has often been noted, in that both documents close with a word of
warning, which is unusual (see the Introduction: 'The nature of the
document'). The warning concerns *one of you* (someone from within
the Christian fellowship) who *strays from the truth*. The idea of stray-
ing rather implies an element of absent-mindedness, as with lost
sheep. But it is stronger and more deliberate than that; there is an
element of deliberate apostasy involved. The writer may have in
mind those who found it difficult to hold on to their Christian
discipleship in the teeth of some of the persecutions envisaged elsewhere in the epistle, but more likely he is thinking of those who fall
by the wayside in a moral or a practical sense. They are said to stray
from the *truth*, but given the context of this writing it is extremely
unlikely that James is implying that they have given way to false
doctrine. This contrast is made elsewhere in the NT (e.g. II Tim.
2.15–18), but not here. Throughout the epistle the author has stressed
that truth is something which is done as well as believed; or perhaps
we should rather say that to believe it *is* to do it (1.18; 2.14–26;
3.13–18). It is a failure to apply the truth to daily living to which our
attention is directed. People like the merchants and traders of 4.13
are meant. But failure is not to be final; why else has the writer
devoted so much of the epistle to encouraging his readers to put
their faith to work? Neither are Christians to be abandoned to their
fate when they begin to *stray*. An important part of what it means to
be part of a Christian congregation is that believers have a God-
given pastoral care for one another. This care can be expressed not
just in the more conventional works of charity, such as looking after
the needy and visiting and praying for the sick, though those are also
commended in this epistle. If the most important thing in life is a
person's response to the Christian gospel, true care will involve
looking after one another in that regard. That this may on occasions
involve brotherly and sisterly correction of one another is known
from the practice of the Matthean community (Matt. 18. 15–17). Nor

is such pastoral care and correction restricted to the 'elders'; if *another succeeds in bringing him back* envisages the possibility of such restorative action being the work of any fellow Christian.

If an erring member is reclaimed, then the one who performs such an action *will be rescuing a soul from death and cancelling a multitude of sins*. Whose soul is this, and whose sins? The Greek is completely ambiguous, and could mean either the soul and sins of the one who is brought back or of the one who is doing the bringing back. REB is right to leave the ambiguity in the English (compare NIV: 'will save him from death'), though in the end there is surely little doubt which is meant. The whole point of the contrast is between someone who requires 'saving' and someone else who, by undertaking the saving action obviously does not require saving him or herself. We must also reject the more complicated suggestion that the soul to be rescued from death is the one who strays, but the *multitude of sins* thereby cancelled belong to the one who is doing the rescuing. If such a thought had been intended there would have been other ways of expressing it. Of course, those who are instrumental in rescuing fellow Christians who have erred are no doubt greatly blessed thereby. Certainly the person who is brought back should be grateful for what has been done, as should the community as a whole. But the soul rescued *from death* is the backslider, and the death from which she or he is rescued is not just physical death but spiritual death, as is shown by the parallel phrase about cancelling (more literally, 'covering') a *multitude of sins* (Rom. 4.7). By being brought back, the sinner experiences repentance and restoration to fellowship with God and with fellow Christians.

James thus brings the epistle to an end, somewhat abruptly, but with the same note of care and concern that his readers should walk in the way of Christian wisdom that has been shown throughout. The Epistle of James may lack the great Christology of Philippians, the soteriology of Romans or the ecclesiology of Ephesians, but it is not after all, an 'epistle of straw'. In its concern for the quality of life of the Christian community, its insistence on the nature of faith as radical obedience and its very practical working out of what it means to be brought to birth by 'the word of truth' (1.18), James offers the church a dynamic for Christian living which it neglects at its peril.

NOTES

Commentaries on the Epistle of James are referred to with full publication details at the first mention in these Notes, but in abbreviated form thereafter, e.g., Ropes, *Commentary*. The two commentaries of P. H. Davids are distinguished from one another by adding (Greek) or (English) as the case may be.

Introduction

1. M. Luther, 'Preface to the New Testament' (1546 edn), *Luther's Works*, ET, Fortress Press, Philadelphia 1960, vol. 35, 362.
2. Ibid, 395.
3. Ibid, 396–7.
4. J. Calvin, *Commentary on the Catholic Epistles*, ET, Eerdmans, Grand Rapids 1948, 276.
5. M. J. Townsend, 'Christ, Community and Salvation in the Epistle of James', *EQ* 53 (1981) 115–23; C. E. B. Cranfield, 'The Message of James', *SJT* 18 (1965), 182–93, 338–45.
6. J. H. Ropes, *The Epistle of St. James*, T.&T. Clark, Edinburgh 1916, 6–18.
7. K. P. Donfried, 'False Presuppositions in the Study of Romans', in K. P. Donfried (ed.), *The Romans Debate*, Augsburg Press, Minneapolis 1977, 120–48.
8. A. Wifstrand, 'Stylistic Problems in the Epistles of James and Peter', *ST* 1 (1947), 170–82.
9. Ibid, 178.
10. W. L. Knox, 'The Epistle of St. James', *JTS* 46 (1945), 10–17.
11. M. Dibelius, *Der Brief des Jakobus* (revised H. Greeven), 11th ed., Vandenhoeck and Ruprecht, Gottingen 1964. ET as *James: A Commentary on the Epistle of James*, Fortress Press, Philadelphia 1976, 3.
12. L. G. Perdue, 'Paraenesis and the Epistle of James', *ZNW* 72 (1981), 241–56, esp. 242–50.
13. P. H. Davids, *The Epistle of James*, Paternoster Press, Exeter 1982, 24.

14. Midrash is a term applied to a certain kind of Jewish exegesis of the scriptures, involving explanation and illustration. It often seems fanciful to those trained in the discipline of historical criticism, but it was carried out according to strict rules and was widely influential. Some scholars have detected a 'Christian midrash' in some parts of the NT.

15. M. Gertner, 'Midrashim in the New Testament', *JSS* 7 (1962), 267–92.

16. R. V. G. Tasker, *The General Epistle of James*, IVP, London 1957, 7.

17. C. L. Mitton, *The Epistle of James*, Marshall Morgan and Scott, Edinburgh 1966, 231–2.

18. C. F. D. Moule, *Worship in the New Testament*, Lutterworth Press, London 1961, 65.

19. D. J. Moo, *The Letter of James*, IVP, Leicester 1985, 38, citing P. H. Davids, *Commentary* (Greek) 23. But Davids is summarizing a doctoral thesis by W.W. Wessel which apparently makes the point that the characteristics often ascribed to the diatribe are equally the characteristics of the Jewish synagogue homily: 'Thus it is as logical to speak of a series of homilies in James as to speak of diatribes.' It is not wholly clear that this supports Moo's overall contention.

20. F. O. Francis, 'The Form and Function of the Opening and Closing Paragraphs of James and 1 John', *ZNW* 61 (1970), 110–26.

21. This German phrase is commonly used by biblical scholars to describe the proper setting and most likely background for a document or tradition.

22. Davids, *Commentary* (Greek), 24.

23. J. B. Adamson, *The Epistle of James*, Eerdmans, Grand Rapids 1976, 20.

24. J. B. Adamson, *James: The Man and His Message*, Eerdmans, Grand Rapids 1989, 113ff.

25. L. T. Johnson, *The Writings of the New Testament*, SCM Press, London 1986, 453.

26. Though this view received strong support from J. B. Mayor, *The Epistle of St. James* (revised 3rd ed.), Macmillan, London 1913, xciii–xcviii, and in modern times from D. Guthrie, *New Testament Introduction*, rev. ed., Apollos/IVP Leicester 1990, 739, who thinks 'Paul is acquainted with a perversion of the kind of teaching which James reflects'.

27. T. Lorenzen, 'Faith without Works does not count before God! James 2:14–26', *ExT* 89 (1978), 231–35, thinks that James does not attack Paul himself, but rather 'a pseudo-Pauline Christianity which has failed to understand Paul's dynamic understanding of faith as total and radical obedience' (233). J. Jeremias, 'Paul and James', *ExT* 66 (1955), 368–71, also supports the idea that James' argument must presuppose Paul.

28. D. J. Moo, *Commentary*, 27–28.
29. See S. Westerholm, *Israel's Law and the Church's Faith*, Eerdmans, Grand Rapids 1988, 16–32 for a summary of their views amongst others.
30. K. Stendahl, *Paul Among Jews and Gentiles*, SCM Press, London 1977, esp. 78–96.
31. E. P. Sanders, *Paul and Palestinian Judaism*, SCM Press, London 1977, 75.
32. Ibid, 421.
33. Ibid, 548.
34. Ibid, 544. For Sanders' own further work on this whole area see his *Paul, the Law and the Jewish People*, SCM Press, London 1985 and *Jewish Law from Jesus to the Mishnah*, SCM Press, London 1990.
35. For a stimulating Jewish response to Sanders' work, see J. Neusner, *Jews and Christians: The Myth of a Common Tradition*, SCM Press, London 1991. The traditional Lutheran view of Paul's theology is argued for very vigorously by H. Hübner, *Law in Paul's Thought*, T.&T. Clark, Edinburgh 1984. For other responses to some aspects of Sanders, see M. D. Hooker, 'Paul and Covenantal Nomism', M. D. Hooker and S. G. Wilson (eds.), *Paul and Paulinism: Essays in Honour of C. K. Barrett*, SPCK, London 1982, 42–56; J. D. G. Dunn, 'The New Perspective on Paul', *BJRL* 65 (1983), 95–122; J. D. G. Dunn, 'Works of the Law and the Curse of the Law (Galatians 3.10–14)', *NTS* 31 (1985), 523–542 and K. Snodgrass, 'Spheres of Influence: A possible solution to the problem of Paul and the Law', *JSNT* 32 (1988), 93–113. A useful overview of the debate can be found in D. J. Moo, 'Paul and the Law in the Last Ten Years', *SJT* 40 (1987), 287–307. Some indication of what the new look in Pauline studies might mean for the way the contemporary church uses one particular Pauline letter can be found in the helpful essay 'Galatians then and now' in J. Ziesler, *The Epistle to the Galatians*, Epworth, London 1992, 105–10.
36. R. J. Fletcher, *The Epistle of James in the Light of New Pauline Studies*, unpublished M.Phil thesis, University of Birmingham 1993, 99.
37. For three relatively recent and contrasting lists, see: W. D. Davies, *The Setting of the Sermon on the Mount*, CUP, Cambridge 1963, 402–3, who suggests that twelve of his listed twenty-five parallels are 'convincing'; P. H. Davids, *Commentary* (Greek), 47–48, who lists thirty-six parallels, plus a further nine 'more general parallels in thought', and P. J. Hartin, *James and the Q Sayings of Jesus*, JSOT Press, Sheffield 1991, 141–2, who offers thirty-one examples. Even within these lists there is anything but unanimity concerning the parallels included by all.

38. J. B. Adamson, *James: The Man and His Message*, 179.
39. So, for example, we might ask whether James 2.15–16 is better paralleled by Matt. 6.25 or by Matt. 25.31–34, both of which have been suggested. The verbal parallels are not strong in either case, but in our judgement the *context* in which James uses the material demands the latter.
40. J. B. Adamson, op. cit., 187. We do not necessarily need to share his strongly held view that the author of the epistle was James the brother of Jesus.
41. M. H. Shepherd, 'The Epistle of James and the Gospel of Matthew', *JBL* 75 (1956), 40–51, esp. 47. Some kind of literary dependence on Matthew is also argued for by B. R. Halston, 'The Epistle of James: 'Christian Wisdom?', *SE* 4 (1968), 308–314.
42. So W. D. Davies, op. cit., 404, following G. Kittel, 'Der geschichtliche Ort des Jakobusbriefes', *ZNW* 41 (1942), 71–105, though Davies (rightly) does not accept Kittel's three-stage scheme for the developing use of the words of Jesus.
43. P. J. Hartin, *James and the Q Sayings of Jesus*.
44. 'Q' is the title given to a collection of the sayings of Jesus (and possibly some other material), in circulation among the early Christian communities prior to the writing of any of our canonical gospels, and on which both Matthew and Luke drew for their work. It probably included a 'nucleus sermon', which may have circulated earlier as an independent unit. There is no absolute unanimity amongst scholars concerning the details of 'Q', and from time time its very existence comes under attack. But there is little doubt that postulating its existence explains a number of otherwise inexplicable things in NT studies.
45. P. J. Hartin, op. cit., 136.
46. Ibid, 195.
47. P. H. Davids, 'James and Jesus' in D. Wenham (ed.), *Gospel Perspectives Volume 5: The Jesus Tradition Outside the Gospels*, JSOT Press, Sheffield 1985, 63–84, 74.
48. P. Carrington, *The Primitive Christian Catechism*, CUP, Cambridge 1940.
49. P. H. Davids, art. cit., 69.
50. J. A. T. Robinson, *Redating the New Testament*, SCM Press, London 1976, 118.
51. P. H. Davids, *Commentary* (Greek), 4, has an incomplete but useful listing of suggested dates.
52. R. J. Fletcher, *James in the Light of New Pauline Studies*, 21.
53. The evidence is very complex. See P. H. Davids *Commentary* (Greek), 28–34, and J. B. Adamson, *James: The Man and His Message*, 228–58,

for full discussions which reach only slightly different conclusions, and S. Laws, *The Epistle of James*, A. & C. Black, London 1980, 6–26, for a radically different assessment.

54. J. A. T. Robinson, op. cit., 120ff.
55. L. T. Johnson, 'James 3:13 – 4:10 and the *Topos Peri Phthonou*', *NovT* 25 (1983), 327–47.
56. J. B. Mayor, *Commentary*, ccvi–cclix. For more modern assessments see A. Wifstrand, 'Stylistic Problems in the Epistles of James and Peter', *ST* 1 (1947), 170–82, who says it was written by one 'who knew ordinary *koine* Greek as it was written by people of some education' but notes semitisms as well, and J. B. Adamson, op. cit., 119–46.
57. J. B. Mayor, op. cit., ccxliv.
58. REB obscures the point by offering the doubtless accurate para- phrase: 'those who spoke Greek' and 'those who spoke the language of the Jews'.
59. F. F. Bruce, *The Acts of the Apostles*, 3rd edn. Apollos, Leicester 1990, 181.
60. On the whole topic see I. H. Marshall, 'Palestinian and Hellenistic Christianity', *NTS* 19 (1973), 271–87.
61. A complex situation is charted in considerable detail by M. Hengel, *Judaism and Hellenism*, ET SCM Press, London 1974. Whatever criticisms may be made of some aspects of his treatment the overall picture is convincing.
62. J. N. Sevenster, *Do You Know Greek? How Much Greek Could the First Jewish Christians Have Known?*, E. J. Brill, Leiden 1968, 190. See also, R. H. Gundry, 'The Language Milieu of First-Century Palestine', *JBL* 83 (1964), 404–8.
63. Ibid, 191.
64. P. J. Hartin, *James and the Q Sayings of Jesus*, 1991.
65. P. H. Davids, *Commentary* (Greek), 33–34.
66. F. F. Bruce, *New Testament History*, rev. ed., Oliphants, London 1971, 356, citing Eusebius, *Ecclesiastical History*, III.5.3.
67. J. A. T. Robinson, *Twelve More New Testament Studies*, SCM Press, London 1984, 108.
68. For a contrary view see, K. L. Carroll, 'The Place of James in the Early Church', *BJRL* 44 (1961), 49–67, who thinks James' blood relationship to Jesus (and descent from David) an important factor.
69. Josephus, *Antiquities of the Jews* XX.9.1 (§ 200).
70. Hegesippus is quoted by Eusebius, *Ecclesiastical History*, II.23.
71. F. F. Bruce, *Men and Movements in the Primitive Church*, Paternoster Press, Exeter 1979, 86–119 has a judicious and perceptive assessment of the role of James in the life of the Jerusalem Church.

72. R.P. Martin, *James*, Word Books, Waco Texas 1988, lxix–lxxvii.
73. Additional reasons for a two-stage theory of composition are given by P.H. Davids, *Commentary* (Greek), 12–13, who argues that it enables us to recover the work's redactional unity.
74. M. Dibelius, *Commentary*, 6.
75. Massey H. Shepherd, 'The Epistle of James and the Gospel of Matthew', *JBL* 75 (1956), 40–51.
76. P.R. Forbes, 'The Structure of the Epistle of James', *EQ* 44 (1972), 147–153
77. J.B. Adamson, *Commentary*, 44–45.
78. P.H. Davids, *Commentary* (Greek), 24–29.
79. P.J. Hartin, *James and the Q Sayings of Jesus*, 1991, 25–33, 244.

Address and greeting (1.1)

1. R. Bauckham, *Jude and the Relatives of Jesus in the Early Church*, T.&T. Clark, Edinburgh 1990, 126–9.
2. These included the growth of what are called the 'Wisdom writings', represented in our OT by Proverbs, Job and Ecclesiastes, and in our OT Apocrypha by The Wisdom of Solomon and Ecclesiasticus (often referred to as 'Wisdom' and 'Sirach'/'Ben Sirach' respectively). The importance of this wisdom tradition for James has long been recognized. For the way in which it developed as a foundation for theology within Judaism, see R.E. Clements, *Wisdom in Theology*, Paternoster Press, Carlisle 1992, 36–39.
3. P. Richardson, *Israel in the Apostolic Church*, CUP, Cambridge 1969.
4. So E.M. Sidebottom, *James, Jude and II Peter*, Nelson, London 1967, 26.

Faith under trial (1.2–27)

1. Paul also uses this term, but less frequently. For example, in Philippians (about the same length as James) it occurs five times. R.P. Martin, *Commentary*, 14, rightly sees it as 'a sign of affection and esteem.
2. H.W. Wolff, *Anthropology of the Old Testament*, SCM Press, London 1974, 186ff.
3. R. Baxter, *The Reformed Pastor* (1656), ed. J.T. Wilkinson, Epworth, London 1950, 139.
4. P.J. Hartin, *James and the Q Sayings of Jesus*, 83.
5. LXX is used to denote the Septuagint, a term which, as commonly understood, describes a translation of the Hebrew Bible into Greek. The name comes from the Latin for seventy, *septuaginta* and

reflects the legend concerning the origin of this version: that it was made by seventy (or rather, seventy-two) 'elders' from the twelve tribes of Israel, brought to Alexandria for the purpose. The real origins are much more obscure and the subject of considerable scholarly debate. The LXX was widely used by Jews in the diaspora who required a Greek translation for synagogue use. It was also the Bible of the early Christian church.

6. J. B. Mayor, *Commentary*, 36.
7. See M. J. Townsend, *Our Tradition of Faith*, Epworth, London 1980, 106–25.
8. E. M. Sidebottom, *Commentary*, 28.
9. A. Carmichael, *Toward Jerusalem* (1936), cited in S. and B. Blanch, *Learning of God: Readings from Amy Carmichael*, SPCK, London 1985, 105.
10. G. von Rad, *Wisdom in Israel*, ET SCM Press, London 1972, 296.
11. K. T. Aitken, *Proverbs*, Saint Andrew Press, Edinburgh 1986, 86.
12. B. R. Halston, 'The Epistle of James: "Christian Wisdom?"', *SE* 4 (1968), 308–14.
13. J. H. Ropes, *Commentary*, 140. R. P. Martin, *Commentary*, 20, says that for James, indecision is the 'hallmark of unbelief'.
14. *Contra* S. E. Porter, 'Is *dipsuchos* (James 1,8;4,8) a 'Christian' Word?', *Bib* 71 (1990) 469–98, who thinks James uses the word in two different ways.
15. P. H. Davids, *Commentary* (Greek), 74–5.
16. See the four articles by O. J. F. Seitz: 'Relationship of the Shepherd of Hermas to the Epistle of James', *JBL* 63 (1944), 131–140; 'Antecedents and Signification of the Term "Dipsuchos"', *JBL* 66 (1947), 211–19; 'Afterthoughts on the Term "Dipsuchos"', *NTS* 4 (1957), 327–34 and 'Two Spirits in Man: An Essay in Biblical Exegesis', *NTS* 6 (1959), 82–95.
17. W. I. Wolverton, 'The Double-Minded Man in the Light of Essene Psychology', *ATR* 38 (1956), 166–75.
18. J. B. Adamson, *Commentary*, 60.
19. W. Barclay, *New Testament Words*, SCM Press, London 1964, 172.
20. There is no evidence for the assertion that 'the poor' was a technical term designating the membership of the Jerusalem (or any other) church on the basis of the well-known OT connection between poverty and piety. See the two articles by L. E. Keck, 'The Poor Among the Saints in the New Testament', *ZNW* 56 (1965), 100–129, and 'The Poor Among the Saints in Jewish Christianity and Qumran', *ZNW* 57 (1966), 54–78.
21. S. E. Johnson, 'The Message of Jesus to the Poor and the Powerful', *ATR* Supplementary Series 11 (1990), 16–28.

22. C. L. Mitton, *Commentary*, 35.
23. The thought-provoking exegesis of P. U. Maynard-Reid, *Poverty and Wealth in James*, Orbis Books, NY 1987, 38–47 is spoiled by a somewhat dogmatic refusal to allow that there could have been any rich Christians in James's community. This is not demanded by the text here, and especially not at 4.13–16.
24. C. H. Dodd, *According to the Scriptures*, James Nisbet, London 1952, 70.
25. J. B. Mayor, *Commentary*, 48–9.
26. E. C. Blackman, *The Epistle of James*, SCM Press, London 1957, 53.
27. See R. C. D. Jasper, *The Development of the Anglican Liturgy 1662–1980*, SPCK, London 1989, 297–8, 349–53.
28. M. Dibelius, *Commentary*, 90.
29. P. H. Davids, *Commentary* (Greek), 80–83.
30. BDB, 428.
31. J. Marcus, 'The Evil Inclination in the Epistle of James', *CBQ* 44 (1982), 606–21, is very helpful on this, though we need not accept his view that the 'evil inclination' underlies 1.2–4 as well as 1.13–15 and 4.5.
32. R. R. Williams, *The Letters of John and James*, CUP, Cambridge 1965, 103.
33. J. Moltmann, *God in Creation*, ET, SCM Press, London 1985, 75.
34. L. E. Elliott-Binns, 'James 1.18: Creation or Redemption?', *NTS* 3 (1956), 148–61, who draws a sharper distinction between Hebraic and Hellenistic ideas than is needed here, with the result that he judges any idea of 'new birth' to be purely Hellenistic, and unnecessary if a Hebraic idea, such as creation, will do instead. The quotation is from 156.
35. See R. Burnish, *The Meaning of Baptism*, Alcuin Club/SPCK, London 1985, esp. 12–13, for the use of some of the NT passages we have cited.
36. D. J. Moo, *Commentary*, 80.
37. F. J. A. Hort, *The Epistle of St James*, Macmillan, London 1909, 38.
38. M. Dibelius, *Commentary*, 113.
39. L. T. Johnson, 'The Mirror of Remembrance (James 1:22–25)', *CBQ* 50 (1988), 632–45.
40. M. J. Evans, 'The Law in James', *VE* 13 (1983), 29–40.
41. Not so oddly as to require us to translate, 'and to protect them in their affliction from the world' on the basis of one 7th century ms: D.J. Roberts, 'The Definition of "Pure Religion" in James 1.27', *ExT* 83 (1972), 215–216.
42. B. C. Johanson, 'The Definition of "Pure Religion" in James 1.27 Reconsidered', *ExT* 84 (1973), 118–19.

Love your neighbour as yourself (2.1–26)

1. In the mss of the Greek NT there are of course no divisions into chapters and verses. Chapter divisions were first introduced into the Latin translation of the Bible in the thirteenth century in order to facilitate referencing. Stephen Langton, who was responsible for this, chose to divide the text into portions of roughly equal length. It just so happens that in *James* the close of the first chapter conveniently coincides with the end of the 'contents list'.
2. So Dibelius, *Commentary*, 130.
3. R.B. Ward, 'Partiality in the Assembly: James 2:2–4', *HTR* 62 (1969), 87–97. See also, P. U. Maynard-Reid, *Poverty and Wealth in James*, 55–61.
4. J. H. Cone, 'Biblical Revelation and Social Existence', *Int* 28 (1974), 425.
5. G. Vermes, *The Dead Sea Scrolls in English*, 2nd ed., Penguin Books, Harmondsworth 1975, 29. The quotation is from the translation of *The War Scroll* 14:7, 142.
6. On this see B.E. Beck, *Christian Character in the Gospel of Luke*, Epworth Press, London 1989, 48–54.
7. From a vast literature see for example V. Caminando, *A Peruvian Catechism*, ET SCM Press, London 1985.
8. So W. Schrage, *The Ethics of the New Testament*, ET T.&T. Clark, Edinburgh 1988, 292. R.P. Martin, *Commentary*, 66, suggests legal pressures over debts, rents, wages and usury.
9. *Contra* J. B. Adamson, *Commentary*, 112–13.
10. R. N. Longenecker, *The Christology of Early Jewish Christianity*, SCM Press, London 1970, 45.
11. G. R. Beasley-Murray, *Baptism in the New Testament*, Paternoster Press, Exeter 1972, 100.
12. Luke (16.17), writing for a non-Jewish readership, gives only a much abbreviated form of this, and sets it in a context (v.16) which suggests a rather different meaning. See also: R. Banks, 'Matthew's Understanding of the Law. Authenticity and Interpretation in Matthew 5:17–20', *JBL* 93 (1974), 226–242.
13. L. T. Johnson, 'The Use of Leviticus 19 in the Letter of James', *JBL* 101 (1982), 391–401.
14. V. P. Furnish, *The Love Command in the New Testament*, SCM Press, London 1973, 179ff.
15. The thesis of M. O'Rourke Boyle, 'The Stoic Paradox of James 2.10', *NTS* 31 (1985), 611–17, that James is here quoting a Stoic paradox in the form in which it is found in Seneca's *De beneficiis*, because the

context in both is the 'reception of gifts without regard to the social status of persons', falls once it it is recognized that the context in James is a commentary upon a passage from Torah, as v.11 makes plain. P. H. Davids, *Commentary* (Greek) 116 lists the Jewish parallels.

16. R. P. Martin, *Commentary*, 69–70, seems to argue that James quotes these because they deal with actual problems in the church.

17. Exod.20.4 = Lev. 19.4; 20.7 = 19.12; 20.8 = 19.3b; 20.12 = 19.3a; 20.15 = 19.11; 20.16 = 19.15b-16a. Lev. 19. 20–22 appears not to be about adultery as such, because in the case of neither party is marital status the point at issue.

18. D. J. Moo, *Commentary*, 98.

19. W. Barclay, *The Plain Man Looks at the Beatitudes*, Fontana, London 1963, 71.

20. P. H. Davids, 'James and Jesus' in D. Wenham (ed.), *Gospel Perspectives Volume 5: The Jesus Tradition Outside the Gospels*, JSOT Press, Sheffield 1985, 75.

21. For a contrary view see, W. Nichol, 'Faith and Works in the Letter of James', *Neot* 9 (1975), 16.

22. R. Y. K. Fung, ' "Justification" in the Epistle of James', in D. Carson (ed.), *Right With God*, Paternoster Press, Carlisle 1992, 146–62, 147.

23. R. J. Fletcher, *The Epistle of James in the Light of New Pauline Studies*, 120.

24. Ropes, *Commentary*, 207.

25. Amongst recent commentators the first of these options is favoured by J. B. Adamson, *Commentary*, 124ff.; the second by R. Y. K. Fung, op.cit. 149–51, and in a modified form by R. P. Martin, *Commentary*, 86–89. The fourth is adopted by by S. Laws, *Commentary* 122–24; P. H. Davids, *Commentary* (Greek), 123–25, D. J. Moo, *Commentary*, 104–6 and G. Stulac, *James*, IVP Leicester 1993, 110 – each with varying degrees of unease. There is no recent support for the third option.

26. C. L. Mitton, *Commentary*, 109.

27. T. Lorenzen, 'Faith without Works does not count before God! James 2:14–26', *ExT* 89 (1978), 232.

28. W. Schrage, *The Ethics of the New Testament*, 282.

29. S. Laws, *Commentary*, 126ff.

30. R. B. Ward, 'The Works of Abraham: James 2:14–26', *HTR* 61 (1968), 283–90.

31. J. A. Ziesler, *The Meaning of Righteousness in Paul*, CUP, Cambridge 1972, 128.

32. Most notably D. J. Moo, *Commentary*, 109.

33. F. F. Bruce, 'Justification by Faith in the Non-Pauline Writings of the New Testament', *EQ* 24 (1952), 76.
34. L. T. Johnson, *The Writings of the New Testament*, SCM Press, London 1986, 459.
35. There is a useful discussion of this aspect in J.G. Lodge, 'James and Paul at Cross-Purposes? James 2,22', *Bib* 62 (1981), 195–213.
36. R. P. Martin, *Commentary*, 97. The view of W. Schrage, op.cit., 289 that the author 'probably cites this example because Rahab is the example of the proselyte, so that there can be no doubt that even for a Gentile there is no possibility of justification except by works', seems something of a *reductio ad absurdum* of his whole argument that James deliberately opposes Paul in this matter.

Christian speaking (3.1–12)

1. Discounting I Tim. 2.7; II Tim. 1.11, where the writer claims teaching as part of the task of an apostle.
2. N. Watson, *The First Epistle to the Corinthians*, Epworth Press, London 1992, 137.
3. F. F. Bruce, *The Epistle to the Colossians, to Philemon and to the Ephesians*, Eerdmans, Grand Rapids 1984, 348.
4. On the subject of the apostolate and its relation to other ministries see R. Schnackenburg, 'Apostles Before and During Paul's Time', in W. W. Gasque and R. P. Martin (eds.), *Apostolic History and the Gospel*, Paternoster Press, Exeter 1970, 287–303.
5. S. Laws, *Commentary*, 143.
6. J. B. Adamson, *Commentary*, 140, strongly disagrees, arguing that the logic is better preserved if James is saying, 'teachers, all teachers, are prone, very prone, to sin.'
7. L. E. Elliott-Binns, 'The meaning of *hylē* in Jas.III.5', *NTS* 2 (1955), 48–50.
8. C. L. Mitton, *Commentary*, 127.
9. M. Dibelius, *Commentary*, 198.
10. *Shabbat* 151b, cited in S. Laws, *Commentary*, 151.
11. Cited by D. J. Moo, *Commentary*, 127, and R. P. Martin, *Commentary*, 117.
12. See for example, the 'Blessings on Various Occasions' in the *Authorised Daily Prayer Book* of the United Hebrew Congregations, 18th ed., Eyre and Spottiswoode, London 1944, 287–92.
13. J. L. Kugel, 'Topics in the History of the Spirituality of the Psalms', in A. Green (ed.), *Jewish Spirituality*, SCM Press, London 1989, 113–44.

The sin of envy (3.13–4.12)

1. L. T. Johnson, 'James 3:13–4:10 and the *Topos Peri Phthonou*', *NovT* 25 (1983), 327–47.
2. W. Barclay, *New Testament Words*, SCM Press, London 1964, 242.
3. We may agree that 'party spirit' is the meaning here, and that there is a link with the situation described in I Cor., without going as far as P. J. Hartin, *James and the Q Sayings of Jesus*, 101 who argues that jealousy has led to party splits within the church and a group has formed under a leader who intends to leave the church in the interests of wisdom and truth. This is to read too much into the phrase.
4. J. A. T. Robinson, *The Body*, SCM Press, London 1952, 9.
5. J. A. Kirk, 'The Meaning of Wisdom in James: Examination of a Hypothesis', *NTS* 16 (1969), 24–38; P.J. Hartin, op. cit., 103–4.
6. S. Laws, *Commentary*, 165–6.
7. C. L. Mitton, *Commentary*, 142. So also, J. Ferguson, *The Politics of Love: The New Testament and Non-Violent Revolution*, Cambridge 1973, 15.
8. L. T. Johnson, op. cit., esp. 336–38.
9. P. J. Hartin, op. cit., 166.
10. On the various groupings see, R.A. Horsley, 'The Zealots: Their Origin, Relationships and Importance in the Jewish Revolt', *NovT* 28 (1986), 159–92.
11. P. W. Barnett, 'Under Tiberius All was Quiet', *NTS* 21 (1975), 564–71.
12. M. Hengel, *Victory Over Violence*, SPCK London 1975, 59.
13. M.J. Townsend, 'James 4.1–4: A Warning Against Zealotry?', *ExT* 87 (1976), 211–13. D. J. Moo, *Commentary*, 141, admits the possibility of this, but states that it does not square well with the indication that the problems were inside the church. However, it is not suggested that the readers were murdering each other, but that some may have been involved with groups which murdered others. This still constitutes a problem within the church! B. Reicke, *The Epistles of James, Peter and Jude*, Doubleday, New York 1964, 45–46, suggests that James is condemning those who by being involved in violent activities placed their fellow-Christians in jeopardy, but the suggestion is made because his dating of the epistle to the persecutions under Domitian about AD 90 necessitates it. The 'Zealot' interpretation is most thoroughly argued by R.P. Martin, *Commentary*, lxiv–lxix, 144ff., who allows that it could well go back to James the Just in a Palestinian setting, but also that it could have had wider application in a different situation and at a later date.

14. K. Grayston, *The Gospel of John*, Epworth, London 1990, 119.

15. J. J. Schmitt, 'You adulteresses! The Image in James 4:4', *NovT* 28 (1986), 327–37.

16. See further, L. T. Johnson, 'Friendship with the World/Friendship with God: A Study of Discipleship in James', in F. F. Segovia (ed.), *Discipleship in the New Testament*, Fortress Press, Philadelphia 1985, 166–83.

17. S. Laws, *Commentary*, 167, 175–79, summarizing an earlier and more extended treatment.

18. F. F. Bruce, *The Canon of Scripture*, Chapter House, Edinburgh 1988, 50–52.

19. J. A. Fitzmyer, *Essays on the Semitic Background of the New Testament*, Geoffrey Chapman, London 1971, 14–15.

20. P. H. Davids, *Commentary* (Greek), 163–4; D. J. Moo, *Commentary*, 145; R. P. Martin, *Commentary*, 150.

21. L. A. Schökel, 'James 5,2 and 4,6', *Bib* 54 (1973), 73–76, sees the citation of Prov. 3.34 as a text to be commented on in the following verses, which is right. However, his interpretation: 'God gives grace to the humble, therefore humble yourselves before God: God opposes the arrogant, you behave arrogantly, should He not oppose you' isolates God's role as judge in the Proverbs quotation.

22. R. P. Martin, *Commentary*, 154.

23. P. H. Davids, *Commentary* (Greek), 169. J. Moffatt, *The New Testament: A New Translation*, rev.ed., Hodder & Stoughton, London 1935, 339, simply transfers this passage to follow 2.13 with a footnote that this 'seems to have been its original place.' The suggestion is entirely sensible, not least because of the importance of Lev.19 both here and in 2.8–13. However, it has no ms authority.

24. L. T. Johnson, 'The Use of Leviticus 19 in the Letter of James', *JBL* 101 (1982), 395.

The danger of wealth (4.13–5.6)

1. P. U. Maynard-Reid, *Poverty and Wealth in James*, 71–77.

2. See J. L. Gonzalez, *Faith and Wealth: A History of Early Christian Ideas on the Origin, Significance and Use of Money*, Harper and Row, San Francisco 1990, 112–18.

3. J. B. Adamson, *Commentary*, 180.

4. C. L. Mitton, *Commentary*, 172–3.

5. The first interpretation is espoused by S. Laws, *Commentary*, 193–4; the second by P. H. Davids, *Commentary* (Greek), 174, and the third by D. J. Moo, *Commentary*, 158, and R. P. Martin, *Commentary*, 168–9.

6. J. B. Mayor, *Commentary*, 154.
7. W. Schrage, *The Ethics of the New Testament*, 292–3.
8. P. U. Maynard-Reid, op. cit., 85ff.
9. So E. C. Blackman, *Commentary*, 144.
10. G. Peck, 'James 5: 1–6', *Int* 42 (1988), 295.

Patience and prayer (5.7–20)

1. G. H. Rendall, *The Epistle of St. James and Judaic Christianity*, CUP, Cambridge 1927, 37.
2. See F. F. Bruce, *Paul: Apostle of the Free Spirit*, Paternoster Press, Exeter 1977, 304ff., for a discussion of this in relation to the Thessalonian church.
3. D. E. H. Whiteley, *The Theology of St. Paul*, Blackwell, Oxford 1970, 233–48 offers a balanced and judicious assessment.
4. J. B. Adamson, *Commentary*, 27.
5. P. H. Davids, *Commentary* (Greek), 187; R. P. Martin, *Commentary*, 194.
6. C. S. Rodd, *The Book of Job*, Epworth Press, London 1990, 6.
7. J. C. L. Gibson, *Job*, Saint Andrew Press, Edinburgh 1985, 9.
8. M. McNamara, *Palestinian Judaism and the New Testament*, Veritas, Dublin 1983, 197–99.
9. C. L. Mitton, *Commentary*, 192.
10. In order to do this with the REB text it is necessary to make certain adjustments. For the sake of clarity, in this version the translation of Matthew has been conformed to that of James in the overlapping parts.
11. P. S. Minear, 'Yes or No: The demand for honesty in the early Church', *NovT* 13 (1971), 1–13. My exegesis is heavily indebted to this excellent article.
12. Justin Martyr, *Apology* 1.16.5.
13. P. S. Minear, op. cit., 6.
14. A. E. Harvey, 'Elders', *JTS* 25 (1974), 318–32.
15. R. P. Martin, *Commentary*, 207, though there incorrectly cited (twice) as 21.28.
16. J. Wilkinson, 'Healing in the Epistle of James', *SJT* 24 (1971), 340.
17. The literature on this subject is considerable. Helpful material, each from different perspectives, may be found in: J. Gunstone, *The Lord is Our Healer*, Hodder and Stoughton, London 1986; J. Wilkinson, *Health and Healing – Studies in New Testament Principles and Practice*, Handsel Press, Edinburgh 1980, and H. Booth, *Healing Is Wholeness*, Methodist Church Division of Social Responsibility/Churches' Council for Health and Healing, London 1987.

18. See H. D. Rack, *Reasonable Enthusiast*, rev. ed., Epworth Press, London 1992, 238ff.
19. P. H. Davids, *Commentary* (Greek), 197.